The Back River Lighthouse at Grandview

Enjoy!
Anna Davids

Ann Davis'

Down by the
BACK RIVER
LIGHT

Illustration by Kym Smith
Photographs from The Daily Press

Morgan James Publishing • New York

Down by the Back River Light

ISBN: 1-60037-130-2 (Paperback)

Published by:

MORGAN · JAMES
THE ENTREPRENEURIAL PUBLISHER
www.morganjamespublishing.com

Morgan James Publishing, LLC
1225 Franklin Ave Ste 325
Garden City, NY 11530-1693
Toll Free 800-485-4943

Habitat for Humanity®
Peninsula
Building Partner

Cover and Interior Design by:
Michelle Radomski
One to One Creative Services
www.creativeones.net

For Hobo and the people he loved.

Acknowledgements

In the preface of Elisha Kane's *Book of Good Love of the Archpriest of Hita*, he said he wished to render thanksgiving to those who contributed to the printing of the work. "Let me sincerely and gratefully but with modesty accord first place to myself," Kane said. I wish to do the same. I accord first place to Elisha Kane. Certainly without him the book, *Down by the Back River Light*, would never have seen the light. This is a story of a most exceptional man.

Secondly, I thank the members of the Kane family for sharing with me. I thank the new owners of Kane Manor for allowing me to roam about the halls and rooms of the old inn on the windy hill in Kane, Pennsylvania.

The Virginiana Room of the Hampton Public Library preserved much information of the trial and the Records Department of the Library of Virginia was also a good resource. Newspaper articles I came across had been clipped from papers from all over the country, but often the source had been clipped away. Therefore, I wish to thank not only the Virginia Peninsula's *Daily Press*, but also all the news people who covered and recorded this story in 1931.

Two professional friends, Mrs. Billie Einseln and Mrs. Judy Credle, gave their services in proofreading the manuscript, highlighting my many grammatical errors, and offering encouraging words. I thank you both.

I thank my husband, Bill Davis, for <u>not</u> holding me beneath the waters of the Chesapeake Bay until I drowned. He may have good reason to do so. It can be difficult to live with a writer so caught up in the past that she doesn't keep up with the present.

I cannot leave out the folks in Hampton who insisted the man was guilty that lured me to investigate the records. I would like to hear from you to know, if after reading this book, it is still your opinion that Elisha Kent Kane, III did willfully and maliciously hold his wife under water until she drowned.

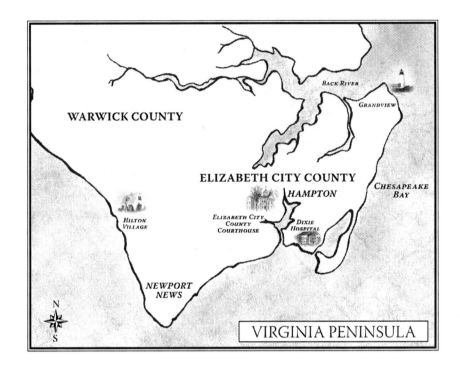

Map of Elizabeth City County

Prologue

My tale took place on the Virginia Peninsula in the third decade of the Twentieth Century.

Like the subjects in Chaucer's *Canterbury Tales*, each character brings to this tale his own perspective. And so I have borrowed Chaucer's style of telling my story by focusing on the personalities as they proceed on their road to Justice. My tale is true. Only two of the subjects you will meet are fictional. They are used to present some background information, but they are of little consequence. The real subjects of *Down by the Back River Light* cannot be upstaged by any I could imagine.

Cover Photography

1) Officer talking to fishermen who will be called as witnesses for the prosecution and the defense
2) The courtroom is packed in anticipation of the trial
3) The jury at the trial
4) Sash Kane being escorted to court by Sheriff Curtis
5) Gravestone at St. John's Cemetery

The Man of Many Tongues

"*W*hat a wretched story! I'm glad the detestable boy got what he deserved, but that poor, poor girl," Molly Fredrick said as they came out of the Tennessee Theatre on Gay Street in downtown Knoxville. The theater's magnificent Wurlitzer pipe organ provided background music for the audience's exodus. They had just seen Josef von Sternberg's adaptation of Theodore Dreiser's book, *An American Tragedy*. The book had caused quite a stir when it came out in 1925. Now, six years later, the movie version was getting controversial reviews.

"He was a blitherin' idiot," Henry Landon said. "If you plan to kill someone, you cover your tracks. He practically advertised he had done it."

"Oh, so it didn't bother you he killed Sylvia Sidney, just that he didn't do a better job of it?" Molly asked.

"The girl was a simpleton," Henry said. "I don't know why Sylvia Sidney took the part."

"That sweet girl had no way of knowing what he intended to do."

"I'm not saying she did," Henry answered. "She was dumb and dizzy to get involved with a man who had to keep their relationship *entre nous*. Where did she expect it to go?"

"She thought he meant what he said," Molly insisted. "Men say anything to get in bed with a woman and, unfortunately, some of us are so naive we believe them."

"Speaking from sexperience?" Henry asked. He was trying to impress Sash Kane, but his manner was rattling Molly who could usually hold her own even in the company of lettered scholars.

She gave him an indignant look. She didn't respond to the question. Instead she turned to Sash, "You haven't said a thing, Sash. What did you think of the movie?"

"Sternberg should be shot," Sash answered.

"Sternberg? But why do you say that?"

"Dreiser's book is supposed to be a study of a man overwhelmed by his circumstances—a man who is forced to do what he does. Sternberg makes the character out to be a fiend."

"Oh-h-h-h, you think Holmes wasn't a fiend? You think he had to kill that innocent girl to shut her up?" Molly asked.

"We'll have to read the book, Molly. The way Sternberg had Holmes play the part you don't see a man under pressure—just a killer. No wonder Dreiser wants to sue Sternberg. He's missed the whole point of what Dreiser was saying."

"Okay, Professor, suppose you tell us how Dreiser could manage to get the reader to sympathize with the man," Henry said. "As I understand it, this really happened. Didn't it?"

"Dreiser based it on the case of a young man, Chester Gillette, who was accused of killing his girlfriend in 1906. He was trying to show that it wasn't in the man's nature to do such a thing, but that Gillette was caught in a dilemma with no way out," Sash explained.

"You mean, like the fellow in the movie who fell in love with Sondra and had to get rid of Roberta because she was pregnant?" Molly asked.

"What I'm saying is we need to read the book," Sash answered. "Dreiser is trying to say that in the end it was an accident."

"I don't buy that," Molly answered. "He got the idea from the newspaper story about a girl's body found in a lake with an upturned canoe. From then on, Clyde thought only of how he could get rid of Roberta."

"Hold your potatoes, Molly. Sash is trying to tell you, the man had a change of heart," Henry said.

"In the movie, he took her to the lake," Molly pointed out.

"Yes, he does," Sash agreed. "But he's still hoping to talk her into going away."

"Didn't he make her ride in a separate train car?"

"He had to. He couldn't afford to have anyone see them together."

"He signed a fake name." Molly said. "Took a picnic basket. Purchased an extra hat. Packed all his belongings in a trunk."

"You're beginning to sound like a prosecutor hungry to convict," Henry said. "Sash's only crime is thinking the movie didn't have the message the author wanted it to have. Ease up."

"Well," Molly said. "Perhaps I should read this book of Dreiser's if he can have his character do all that and still suggest it might have been an accident."

"I have to read the book myself. But I understand that Dreiser shows Clyde couldn't go through with it when the time came," Sash said. "He realized what he was about to do... before Roberta stood up and came towards him. He didn't mean for her to fall."

"But he knew she couldn't swim," Molly said. "He could have saved her. Oh, it was so terrible! The panic on that poor girl's face when she realized he meant to let her drown. I couldn't believe he'd do that. And then they showed that cute little hat of hers floating in the water."

"I wonder if it was an accident," Henry said. "I suppose the truth will never be known."

"Chester Gillette got the electric chair for the drowning death of Grace Brown," Sash said. "Dreiser went to the penitentiary to see him before he died."

"Perhaps that's where he got the idea that it was not in the man's 'nature' to do such a thing," Molly said. "Perhaps you're right. But the way the movie showed it, the man was nothing but a fortune-seeking, self-centered villain. Did you see the look in his eyes when he read the newspaper article? He lured her to the lake with a picnic lunch. He should have choked on his sandwich! I used to think Phillips Holmes was good looking—sort of 'momma's little boy' type—but I don't know that I could stand to watch him on the screen again."

"I'll never forgive him for drowning Sylvia Sidney," Henry said. "I couldn't endure the character Frances Dee played. Of course she was pretty, but featherbrained. Clyde soaked up all her 'Clydie-bydie-sweetums' talk. I'd never let any woman call me by such lovey-dovey names in front of other people."

"Henry," Molly said, "has any woman ever had an affectionate name for you?"

"Sondra may have been a bit flighty," Sash said, smiling at his two companions, "but she had potential. Once Clyde married her, his days of struggling to be somebody would be over. He would have wealth and position. With Roberta, he would have been doomed to a life as a destitute as his father had been. He wanted nothing more than to get away from the poverty he was born into."

"He was so ashamed of his sister when she went off and got pregnant, but he put Roberta in that same situation," Molly said.

"I'm sure Dreiser wrote the story showing Clyde rethinking what happened to his sister. All through the book, Clyde is supposed to be trying to come to terms with life. He was too smart to be a mere laborer. He could have been anything his cousin was if only he had had the same opportunities. While Cousin Gil was going on pony rides, Clyde was on the streets in St. Louis, practically a beggar."

"In the movie, he could have done all right for himself had he not been so indifferent," Molly said. "Oh, he was simply stuck up—teasing women like he was too good for them."

"I'm sure Holmes did not play the character of Clyde like Dreiser wrote it. That's the author's complaint. Get the book. I will, too," Sash said. "Then we'll have this discussion. I'm certain Dreiser will make you look at it all differently.

"I never tell the truth, when a lie can be more entertaining."

— *Elisha Kent Kane*

"Shall we go somewhere for a nightcap?" Henry asked.

"No. I mean I don't have time tonight," Molly said. "A couple of Professor Martin's students turned in their term papers late. I'll be up all night reading—but not Dreiser."

"Then I'll drop you by your place," Henry said. Sash rushed ahead to open the car door for her.

Sash climbed in the back seat of Henry's sedan. Henry wondered why Sash hadn't driven his sporty roadster he had seen him in on campus. Henry felt a bit embarrassed by the vehicle he was driving.

"Well, Henry," Sash shouted from the backseat, "Do you let your students get away with tardy work?"

"It's always been my policy to offer to let them turn things in the following year when they repeat the course, if you get my drift," Henry said.

"Oh, I get your drift." Sash laughed. "I suspect they do, too."

Professor Elisha Kent Kane, called Sash by his friends, was relatively new to the campus. He was a nice-looking young man. Henry had heard he had attended Cornell University and earned his Ph.D. from Harvard. He was from a prominent Pennsylvania family. Young, very tall, some would say handsome (though he had a rather large nose), probably rich, and already distinguished as holding the chair of his department at Tennessee U. Henry had preferred to avoid Professor Kane. He'd wondered, as he watched from a distance, if Kane wasn't a bit too familiar with the students. At times Henry noticed coltish coeds flirting with the man. *But that doesn't mean he encourages them,* he told himself.

This afternoon Molly, a staff assistant, had phoned Henry asking him to go to the theater with her and Sash. She and this other professor had been talking about the movie that was playing and, well, she wanted to see it, but didn't feel right going with just Sash. "It might not look right. His wife is out of town, you know. Oh, and can you drive?"

Henry didn't particularly care to see *An American Tragedy*—not his idea of entertainment. He was a professor of mathematics and more inclined to James Cagney gangster films that didn't require a degree in psychology to figure them out.

"His wife's family lives in Tidewater. Maybe he knows someone at Hampton Institute," Molly suggested.

"It's too late to be asking questions, Molly. I'm committed. Tennessee's budget cuts were going to leave me jobless soon. I'll be better off in the private school."

"I hate to see you leave," Molly said. "But you could at least go out with us tonight."

Henry agreed, "Yes, and I'll drive."

When Molly got out of the car, Sash walked her to her door before coming back to sit in the passenger's side of the front.

"Now, how about a whiskey, Professor?" Henry asked.

"I'd like that very much, Henry. But where are we going to get whiskey?"

"I know a couple of hillbillies—flunked out of my class a few years ago. But we've kept up a friendship, you might say."

"I've been here at Tennessee U. for two years," Sash said, "but I don't feel I've had an opportunity to get to know some of you on the faculty as I should."

"I must apologize," Henry said, guilty of having made no effort to welcome the new professor. "I should have…"

"Oh, no," Sash interrupted. "I am the one who is at fault. What I mean is, my wife has been spending a great deal of time in Virginia at the home of my in-laws. I haven't been very social. I'm afraid I bury myself in my studies when she's gone."

"I understand. I do hope your wife…?" He paused for Sash to fill in the name.

"Jenny."

"Yes, I do hope Jenny will be able to stay here next semester and you can get to know more folks. I am leaving…"

"I hope so too, Henry." Sash answered without hearing all of what Henry said. "Jenny and I have moved around a great deal. We've been from North Carolina, to Miami, and then to Tennessee."

"It's quite a plume in your helmet—you hold the chair in the Romance Language department," Henry said, wondering what it was about Sash that he had so easily fallen into the position. "Tennessee was very lucky to get you."

"'Your sentiments are noble but—kind words no biscuits butter.' Still, I consider myself lucky to be here. You see, I am quite enthralled with my studies. At present I'm working on a translation of *El Libro de Buen Amor* by Juan Ruiz."

"Run that by me again. I'm afraid my Spanish is a little rusty." Henry parked the car in front of his apartment and the two of them walked to the door. "I never was good at foreign languages. Do you speak Spanish fluently?"

"Languages are easy for me. I'm fluent in seven. But," Sash added, "the language of mathematics, the one you have mastered, leaves me cold."

"What is it that you're translating?" Henry asked Sash. "A Spanish love story?"

"It means 'The Book of Good Love.' Juan Ruiz has been called the Spanish Chaucer," Sash explained.

"Hmmm," Henry thought of this a minute. "Then 'Good Love' doesn't necessarily mean virtuous."

"'This book is like an instrument, to every tune it's true; your heart it is which makes the song seem merry, sweet, or blue.'" Sash quoted a rhyme from the book. "You're right though, Juan Ruiz was the Archpriest of Hita, but it isn't the sort of book you'd expect from a churchman. Some say it is downright vulgar."

"And you think we need this translated into English?" The two men entered Henry's apartment. What the place lacked in décor, it made up for in stacks of frayed boxes. Henry poured two glasses of whiskey and handed one to Sash.

"Yes, I do, and I'll tell you why. Ruiz is trying to distinguish between sacred and romantic love. The Spanish believed strongly in the church, but they recognized their church leaders as human beings not above reproach. Ruiz tells of a clergyman who gets involved with a woman. His writing is full of Spanish wit. He makes wide use of play on words. He's really quite remarkable for his time. As the Archpriest says, 'No word is wicked in itself unless it's wrongly taken.'"

"My reading library favors lighter reading," said Henry. "*Look Homeward, Angel*, by Thomas Wolfe is the most literary book I've tackled lately. I prefer the Sunday comics."

"*Look Homeward, Angel* is not a bad read," said Sash. "I don't suppose I could interest you in reading my book? I'll even autograph it. If you'll read it."

"Something tells me, it's not my kind of story," Henry said hesitating. "Is it illustrated?"

"Yes, I illustrated it myself. I titled it *Gongorism and the Golden Age—A Study of Exuberance and Unrestraint in the Arts.*"

"Then I wouldn't get past your pompous title," Henry said.

"How about trying Dreiser's *An American Tragedy*?" Sash asked. "It will make you think."

"If I'm going to think, I'd rather think about something other than why a man killed a woman." Henry refilled their glasses. "No, I leave such ponderous reading for you and Molly to discuss. So, I'm told your grandfather was the Arctic explorer..."

"No, that was my great-uncle for whom I am named. He had a theory that much of the northern hemisphere had once been covered with ice. He died when he was just thirty-seven—as old as I am now—but he proved his theory. He was right."

"To bite the dust when he was just thirty-seven—he couldn't have explored much in such a short time. Did he die in the Arctic?"

"No, he died in bed," Sash said. "Uncle Elisha packed a lot of living into his brief life. From childhood until he died after a couple of strokes, my uncle suffered numerous illnesses—rheumatic fever, cholera, typhus, you name it—he had it. Illness may have slowed him down, but he didn't let it stop him. He traveled the world. He fought in the Mexican War and was wounded. Adversity constantly challenged him. He and his crew were lost at sea, or trudging through blinding snow..."

"I get the point. The man didn't have it easy," Henry said.

"But he wasn't all work and no play, no sir," Sash added. "There was a girl named Julia Reed. Just as it seemed he would settle down, he signed on for a tour of duty in Africa. Funny thing was Julia was pregnant when he suddenly scheduled his own disappearance. Still, it was his other love affair that became public knowledge."

"Why, was this one married to someone else?"

"If that were only all it was," Sash said. "No, this woman, Margaret Fox, was a spiritualist. She and her sister claimed they could communicate with the dead through a series of peculiar rappings. Uncle Elisha started going to the hotel where they held séances when he was particularly depressed.

"Margaret and Katherine had started this as a joke. A gullible public was taken in, and the girls saw they had a lucrative enterprise. They had double-jointed toes which they could crack at will to emanate the noises they claimed were coming from the dead. But my uncle and Maggie's friendship developed into a relationship that developed into something of a scandal—a Kane involved with the likes of her!"

"I hope he didn't stop seeing her," Henry said, finding Sash's story amusing.

"He recognized the fraud and told her that if she'd give up her toe-cracking and get an education, he could marry her. He paid for her education, but when the time came, the highfalutin' Kane family wouldn't allow the marriage."

"From what you've told me, Professor, your uncle got seriously ill all over the globe and had a couple of scandalous affairs..."

"But you can't forget, Professor Landon, my uncle was a hero. He was known the world over as the great Arctic explorer. His name is in history books."

"And what legendary thing do you intend to do so that the name Elisha the Third will also be in the history books?" Henry asked and then wondered at his own audacity.

But Sash answered him with humor, "What is there for me to do? My grandfather commanded the Pennsylvania 'Bucktail' Regiment in the Civil War. Grandma Bessie was one of Pennsylvania's first female physicians. My father was a sensation when he took out his own appendix. He's in the medical textbooks."

"Ah, yes, it was in the newspapers back when I was a student. Got a lot of publicity," said Henry, raising his bushy eyebrows and twisting the right curl of his mustache, (a habit he couldn't break). "He performed an appendectomy on himself. Something I always wished I could do."

"Do I detect sarcasm from my colleague?" Sash asked.

"Well, I don't like to take out my own false teeth, let alone a body part. Perhaps it's envy you detect." Henry enjoyed this exchange of levity. He liked Sash Kane.

"If you're inclined to envy me, try this. I was born in Kane, Pennsylvania. The town was founded by my grandfather. Imagine being a kid named after the famous explorer, Elisha Kent Kane, in the small town of Kane. It was worse than being the preacher's son."

"I see what you mean, but you seem to have come through it without any scars," Henry said, thinking his own accomplishments very slight by comparison.

"I'm the black sheep of the family."

"Aristocratic poppycock! What do they expect of you? You're a Ph Demon."

"... in a very small college," Sash said. "I'm supposed to make headline news across the nation. My father and I don't think alike. He says I'm disrespectful of all that's been given to me. I owe something to the Kane family name, and I'm not likely to attain it studying romance languages."

"Let's have one more drink," Henry said pouring his own, "but this is my limit. Will you be in Hampton for a while, Sash?"

"I'll be heading to Ft. Bragg before I can go on to the oceanside."

"You're in the Reserves?"

"Yes, sir. Jenny thinks I enjoy it too much."

"Do you?"

"Perhaps. But Jenny's just impatient for me to come to Virginia for her. She says Hobo is always looking for me."

"Hobo?"

"Our German Shepherd. Hobo's father was a movie star in the silent films."

"Not Rin Tin Tin?" Henry asked.

"No, his name was Strongheart. He was the first German Shepherd of the silver screen and he got the lead part. He died a couple of years ago. The newspapers said he just died at home, but I was told he'd been injured on the set—got a bad burn when he fell against a hot studio light and died a few weeks later. He wasn't just a pup. He was thirteen when he died. He was a magnificent animal, and he was a good actor."

"Didn't the Hollywood trainers want your dog for the movies?"

"Hobo?" Sash shook his head. "It's a good thing they didn't try to make an actor out of him. Hobo can act hungry, but that's it. I tell my students I miss my dog, my car and my wife, in that order," he laughed, "but, Henry, just between us, I think Jenny really does favor Hobo over me or my car."

"She must love to swim," Henry said. "I mean growing up on the coast I can't blame her for wanting to be there for the summer."

"Jenny's just learned to swim. She's always been afraid to get her head wet. Sounds sort of cockeyed for someone from the coast. She's been taking lessons from a swimming instructor in Newport News."

"It has to be hard to learn to swim at her age. I mean, it's much easier to teach a child," Henry said.

"My wife had no confidence in herself. She had some trauma when she was a child—nothing all that serious, but she's had a terrible time overcoming her fear of the water. "

"I heard your wife sing at a university function. She is quite talented," Henry said.

"Yes, she is. She studied at the Conservatory of Music in Boston. And she's a painter. We often go on sketching excursions together.

Her art is more sentimental than mine. I tend to do caricatures."

"Y-y-y-yes," Henry said recalling. "You did an article for the *News-Sentinel* and you did a self-caricature. I must say you weren't very kind to yourself."

"I'm the perfect subject for the caricature artist with this very long, curved nose. At least, as an artist, I can make the best of it."

Henry tipped his glass to get the last drop of his whiskey. "Well, Professor Kane, it's been pleasant getting to know you. You're a very interesting chap. Now, I'll drive you home. I must check in on my mother soon. She expects a call every night."

"'What can't be cured must be endured,'" quoted Sash as he followed Henry to the door.

Henry puzzled over the remark. "Oh, but I won't be enduring this much longer. I'm leaving Knoxville."

"Well, I'm sorry to hear that, Henry. I was hoping I might talk you into doing some hiking in the mountains with me. There are a few of us at the university who do weekend hiking trips. Good, clean mountain air. It would've been good for you. Jenny used to go, but she can't exert herself too much. She gets these spells."

"That so? Too bad," Henry answered. "I've never been tempted to go mountain climbing. If they haven't built a road up to the top, I can wait until they do. My sport is baseball, and I do that sitting in the stands screaming at the umps. Have you ever been to the World Series?"

"Can't say that I have," Sash replied. "I'm not big on spectator sports. I played a little hockey when I was in school. You can let me out here."

Henry stopped the car at the Kingston Manor Apartments.

"I appreciate your driving me all the way out here, Sash said. "I keep telling Jenny I should get a place closer in, but she thinks I need all the space I have here."

"Glad to do it, my friend," said Henry. "I'm glad you and Molly got me out. A morbid movie, but I enjoyed it just the same. Goodnight."

Henry drove off realizing he hadn't asked Sash about Hampton Institute, but as he told Molly, it was late to be asking questions now. *I wonder where Sash's roadster is.*

The Fair Lady

*H*ilton Village, Virginia, was a self-contained community built in 1918 for the shipyard workers during The War. It was just north of Newport News, above the shipyard along the polluted James River. It looked like a quaint English village—the houses painted white or creamy yellow with brown trim. Hilton Village had a village green, shops, a bank, a theater and Seward's Grocery with its stacks of fresh produce in bushel baskets out front.

The streetcar ran down the center of Warwick Road. The Graham home was at the corner of Post Street and Warwick. There were single-family homes and "half-of-a-double(s)" and "three-of-a-triple(s)," all having at one time been owned by the shipyard. After The War, people were permitted to buy the homes. One of the prestigious singles with its side-gabled, steeply sloped slate roof was the home of the bespectacled Magistrate, Walter C. Graham. A dormer with double windows was above the center front door of the frame house.

In her parents' home, Elisha Kane's wife of thirteen years was reading the tragic story of the life of Isadora Duncan, a book she had asked Sash to send her. In September of 1927, Jenny had been horrified by news reports of the accidental death of the famous dancer.

In an interview, Isadora had told the *Associated Press* correspondent, "I am frightened that some quick accident might happen."

"She knew something was going to happen, Sash," Jenny said, reading from the newspaper article several years ago. "At last it seemed that she could pull herself out of debt, but she knew something was going to go wrong. She said so the day before she died."

"My dear Babe, you are crying. You are such a sentimental fool," Sash said.

"I suppose I am," Jenny admitted, "but the way she died was ghastly."

"I didn't take time to read the story," Sash said. "What happened?"

"It says: 'Miss Duncan was hurled in an extraordinary manner from an open automobile in which she was riding and instantly killed.' Then it goes on to say a loose end of the scarf she had wrapped around her got caught in the rear wheel of the car. 'The scarf of strong silk,' Jenny read again from the paper, 'suddenly began winding around the wheel and with terrific force dragged Miss Duncan, around whom it was securely wrapped, bodily over the side of the car... She was dragged for several yards before the chauffeur halted.' Oh, what a cruel death!" Jenny said, dropping the paper onto the floor.

"From what I understand, life had not been kind to Isadora Duncan," Sash said. "At first she made a fortune with her interpretative dancing. Then, she shocked the pants off the critics when she started dressing in costumes of translucent material. She wasn't well received in America, but she did do well in Paris... until her two children were killed in an auto accident, I think. From then on, it seemed bad fortune was her lot."

"Oh, Pappy," (Jenny and Sash often called each other by adoring names) "I want to read all there is to read about her."

"She wrote an autobiography. I'll try to find it for you," Sash answered. "She was a defender of the poetic spirit, something I believe in."

"And I'm quite certain my husband found her translucent costumes... interesting?"

The Graham house in Hilton Village at the corner of Warwick Avenue and Post Streets

"It was her way of expressing her art," Sash replied with a smile.

The more Jenny learned of Isadora, the more provocative the woman proved to be.

As Jenny read the book Sash had mailed a short time ago, her tear-filled eyes distorted the words she tried to read. Though Isadora Duncan was certainly a revolutionist, she displayed a capacity for love and compassion that Jenny found phenomenal. When the driver of the car that had caused the deaths of her children came to see her, Isadora assured him that she knew it was an accident and told him to go home to his children. She organized dancing schools in several countries. Isadora chose to offer lessons to children who could not afford to pay. Though debts plagued her, she provided for all their needs. Isadora had several lovers, but the one man she married, a poet much younger than she, was subject to fits of epilepsy. He ended his own life by cutting his wrists and writing a poem in his own blood.

Still, all that Jenny learned of Isadora only reminded her of the dancer's premonition. Jenny felt a kinship to this woman who had danced in flowing tunics—with free and natural movements. Jenny had a premonition of her own death.

While eagerly waiting for her husband, Jenny spent a lot of time upstairs in her room. She would read and reread chapters of the book while visualizing the famous dancer at the Bolshoi Theatre in Moscow leaping across the stage with flowing scarves stretched behind her feminine form. Then Jenny would stand before a mirror wrapped in the sheet from her bed, striking an Isadora pose. She'd hum the music of the great composers Isadora loved to perform with and dream that Sash was there laughing with her.

In the morning her mother would tap on the door to her room and call, "Jenny, you mustn't keep yourself confined in there. Come on down and get something to eat."

Mrs. Graham was concerned about her daughter's loss of appetite. "You don't eat enough to keep a bird alive," she'd tell her. "No wonder you feel so out of kilter. There's nothing wrong with you that a hearty breakfast of bacon, eggs, biscuits and gravy wouldn't cure. Please, come on down, Honey."

Jenny would listen as her mother walked away. She'd tried to tell her mother she got nauseated when she ate greasy foods. Jenny and Sash had learned to eat differently. The rich foods her mother prepared didn't settle well on her stomach.

"Nonsense! You are fading to a frazzle. Are you worried about something? Come on, child, eat up. Put some meat on your bones."

Mr. Graham thought Jenny's eating habits critical of her mother's cooking. He'd leave the table saying he wouldn't sit there and watch her pick at her food. "Your mother is an excellent cook."

Jenny found it easier to pretend she was sleeping than to join the family at the table. Still, she did get hungry, but with the tight budget she and Sash had had to endure that summer, she often skipped meals altogether.

Jenny felt somewhat to blame for their financial predicament. She had been putting things on account willy-nilly before Sash finally sat down with her and showed her their debts had gotten out of hand. "Ernst sent me a notice threatening collection for his $30.00, and the music store is getting impatient," Sash told her.

"I'm going to have to work the summer school session, Babe. It won't be much of a summer vacation for you."

"You were going to teach me to swim," said Jenny. "I've been thinking positive thoughts about it. I was determined to learn to swim this summer so I could swim with you. And we would picnic on the beach and have another jellyfish war like we had last year."

"Babe, I have to get us out of debt. There'll be no long vacation this year, but we'll plan a big trip before the fall semester. It gets really hot here during the summer—we're further south, and we don't get any ocean breeze. It's going to be pretty miserable. Perhaps you'd like to go to Virginia and stay with your folks."

Jenny had chosen to stay with her folks in Hilton Village when Sash had taken a job in Madrid, Spain, several years after they were married. The thought of crossing the ocean scared Jenny. In fact, though Jenny wanted to be adventuresome, she often allowed her anxieties to limit her activities.

"I don't want to have to live without you again, Pappy. And all summer. Couldn't you do something in Virginia?"

"Jobs are hard to come by right now, Babe. I'm lucky to get a contract here," Sash answered. "But our one little fan isn't going to keep this place cool. Administration says they will have two classes for me to teach. That will bring in $400.00 for each six-week session. I should be able to get these bills out of the way and afford a nice trip at the end of the summer."

"I'm sorry, Pappy. I didn't realize…"

"It's not your fault, Babe. The University cut salaries. We just didn't adjust. I'm not good at budgeting myself—never learned how."

"I want you to go to the beach everyday," Sash told Jenny before she left Tennessee.

"It doesn't seem fair," Jenny replied. "You're the one who loves to swim."

"I can find a pool here. We'll have a tan war," he said, "—see which of us has the deepest tan at the end of the summer. And I want you to take the roadster."

"But..."

"No buts. If you have the car, you can get to the beach. You need the cool sea air. And I suppose you might as well take Hobo along. He'd be bored sick stuck here alone with me. I'll be working on the translation. If I get it finished, it could put some money in our piggybank. You can take him when you go to Grandview. He loves it there."

Jenny vowed she would learn to swim during the summer. She took lessons from Dr. Vanderslice's son. She was relieved he refused to let her pay him. Jenny's letters to Pappy told of her progress with her swimming lessons. "I can swim on my back and side."

He wrote Jenny of the progress he was making with interpreting *The Book of Good Love*—"I've typed over 1300 stanzas of 1700." He told her the university cancelled one of his classes, and that reduced his summer income by one hundred and fifty dollars.

She wrote Sash she received the cigarettes he sent. She told him she had a bout with shingles.

He paid for the piano. "Now it is yours for good," he wrote.

"I'll never leave my Pappy again," she wrote him. "I'm homesick for my Pappy. I received Isadora Duncan and the other book you sent," she said.

In July he wrote Jenny, "I got a new summer suit from the complex so that I could wear it while the other was cleaned. I'm sending you ten dollars. I want you to build up and get a strong body."

"In just a month, by the time you get this letter," Sash wrote, "I will be with you again."

"Three weeks, I'll be with you," she wrote. "I'm taking good care of Hobo, but he misses you. I say everyday, 'Where's Pappy?' Hobo looks everywhere—his ears up."

"I can swim now. I'm not afraid of the water."

— *Jenny G. Kane*

"I think at night how wonderful it would be for us to be on the beach," Sash wrote. "It is a pity that we all three have to get old. I wish the sunshine past would come back again. Why didn't you go to the beach?" he asked. "I want you to breathe the cool sea air."

"You are so good and have to work all summer," she said. "and I feel so bad to go to the ocean when you can't go."

"I think of my baby all the time and wonder what you're doing," he wrote.

"I can swim well now," she bragged. "I'm not afraid of the water."

"Oh, I'm so proud of my baby," he answered. "My book will soon be done—all but the illustrations," he said.

"My baby works so hard," Jenny wrote. "I'm so selfish, but I don't mean to be."

"I want us to go to Grandview," he wrote, "for I want to see whether I can still swim from the inlet down to the lighthouse as I used to do so many times. After the camp, we'll have nearly two weeks till school opens, so I would like to go up home very much to see Gramps," Sash wrote.

"I have a little cold," she told him. "You'll enjoy the camp."

"I love my babe," he answered.

After a rainy week in August, Jenny felt sure she would lose the tan war, but she wanted Sash to hold her in his loving arms even if he would win the tanning competition. Sash was the only one who understood her. Others accused her of being a hypochondriac, but Sash took her seriously. Jenny had spells when it felt like her heart had stopped. Doctors said they couldn't find anything wrong. Even Sash's father had gotten impatient with her once he examined her and couldn't find anything to cause her spells. But Sash would put his ear to her heart, trying to detect her irregular heartbeat. Sometimes they'd sleep all night like that—his head on her breast while he calmed and reassured her. He insisted that she not get over-stressed, that she eat foods that weren't so rich, that she breathe fresh air… he treated her like a fragile china doll. Jenny missed his doting.

Sash phoned Jenny from Norfolk. He'd gotten there a day sooner than they'd expected. "Can you come over here for me?" he asked.

"Oh, Pappy! It's wonderful. You're home. Yes. Yes, of course I'll come for you. As soon as I can get there. Pappy, you're home early."

"I thought I'd surprise you. How about our having dinner over here tonight?" he asked. "We can go to the Cavalier at the beach. I can't wait to see my Babe."

The Bereaved Brother

O n the morning of September the eleventh, Dr. George Vanderslice went by Dixie Hospital to look in on a pneumonia patient. The doctor's goateed chin, salt and pepper hair, and very erect and dignified stance combined to suggest the respect he received at Dixie. He was the surgeon on staff at the hospital. He had opened his medical practice in Phoebus thirty-eight years ago and had been the county coroner for twenty-eight years.

"We have just phoned for you for a coroner's case, Dr. Vanderslice," Hazel Wells called to him when he was partly up the stairs to the second floor.

"All right, what is the case?"

"The poor woman drowned," Mrs. Wells said. "Her husband brought her in about a half hour ago. The man is grief-stricken. He kept begging us to get another doctor—someone who could save her. The pulmotor wasn't working properly, but I don't think it would have helped. She was already dead when he brought her in."

Dr. Vanderslice came back down the stairs. "Elisha Kane, and his wife, Jenny," Mrs. Wells whispered to the physician as she pointed to the tall professor.

"Mr. Kane, I am Dr. Vanderslice. I want to express my sympathies to you..."

Sash, standing in the hallway where the hospital was undergoing some new construction, turned around and shook his head. The doctor approached the very tall and very tanned young man who was wearing a dark bathing suit and one sock.

"... and I'll need you to answer some questions so I can fill out the necessary papers."

Sash straightened himself up, "It is hard for me to believe, Doctor," he sucked in a big breath. "She was doing well and then, it all happened before I could do anything."

"What happened, Mr. Kane?"

"We had gone to Grandview. We often went down by the lighthouse. We had been swimming and playing in the water, when we decided to stop to have our picnic lunch. Jenny was getting the things out. I decided to swim out a ways alone while she was doing that. I told her to watch me. I swam out, I don't know, about two hundred and fifty to three hundred yards, and I turned because I thought I heard her calling to me. Just as I turned, she dove, or slipped, from the rocks by the lighthouse into the water. I knew she was in trouble—she screamed as she disappeared from sight. I swam as hard as I could to get to her."

"Do you think possibly her foot slipped from a rock and caught in a crevice between that rock and another?" Dr. Vanderslice asked.

"I don't know. I thought she was telling me to watch her. I thought she was practicing her diving. Maybe her foot slipped. When I got to her, the water had taken her out beyond her depth, and I tried to get a hold of her; but first she pulled me down with her. Finally, I was able to get her back to the rocks. I was exhaust-ed. I hollered for help. There were fishermen close enough to hear me, but no one came. I knew I had to get her to the hospital. So I backed the car down onto the beach and put her in it and drove as fast as I could."

"Do you live around here?"

"If Jenny ever went into the water that was deep enough she could drown, she was carried there."

— *Hop Graham*

"No. I'm a professor at the University of Tennessee. This was only a vacation."

"I see."

Dr. Vanderslice proceeded to fill out a death form with the information Sash had given him. He filled out two, as the law required. One he would keep for his own information. He assumed, as the Kanes were out-of-towners, it was necessary to get the papers ready so the body could be moved to Tennessee. The woman's husband wouldn't be able to have the body moved without a statement from him.

Dr. Vanderslice left Sash sitting in a small waiting area. "If you need anything, Mr. Kane, ask Mrs. Wells," he said placing his hand on Sash's shoulder, a gesture of sympathy.

The evening of the next day, Hop Graham, Jenny's brother, visited Dr. Vanderslice. "Dr. Vanderslice," he began, "when my brother-in-law brought my sister's body to Dixie Hospital, did you do an investigation of the cause of death?"

"Mr. Kane said Jenny had slipped. I didn't realize who she was at the time. I accepted his statements. I think it was an accidental death," the doctor answered.

Hop stood in the doctor's office twisting his hands and trembling a little.

"Why, Hop? What is troubling you?"

"Did you look her over completely… thoroughly, I mean?"

"Sit down, Hop. Now, why do you ask these questions?" Dr. Vanderslice asked.

"Doctor, my sister and her husband weren't getting along. There was another woman. We have letters she's written him. He was interested in this other woman. Then he takes Jenny down on the isolated beach where there's no one to see what he does to her and brings her back and tells some cockeyed story that don't add up. I heard he passed out at the hospital. He pulled a phony on them at the hospital—that's what he did. "

"You don't think it was an accident? You think Kane killed your sister?"

"Well," Hop said, "I think he wanted to get rid of her. I'm saying something isn't right. He keeps changing his story. First, he tells someone he was on the beach; then he tells someone else he was far out in the water. I tell you, something ain't right."

"There didn't appear to be any bruises on Jenny, Hop. The man had a look of intense agony when I saw him. He appeared to be quite shaken by the incident."

"It's an act. He's glad she's dead. He didn't want to have to put up with her bellyaching anymore," Hop insisted.

"I tell you what," the doctor said, "being as you're a fisherman down at Newcomb's place, perhaps you could ask around. Find out if anyone saw anything. Could you do that? You could bring me their names. Then I could call them in to see me."

"I could do that."

"And I'd like to take a look at those letters you mentioned, Hop. If this wasn't an accident, like the man said, I will find out."

"Yes, sir. Thank you, Dr. Vanderslice. I think you'll find these letters very interesting. The woman comes right out and suggests that Sash get rid of his wife. I'll be back with what you need."

Other coroners would have handed the case over to county detectives. Dr. Vanderslice was inclined to keep at a case to solve any mystery that might exist. The doctor saw it not only as his duty—it was his hobby. He was known to be meticulous. He had proven his abilities many times over.

A kimono, bathing suit, hat and lunch box were found on the beach near the lighthouse by officers investigating the area where the drowning took place. They were said to have belonged to the professor and his wife.

The Eyewitnesses

*T*he following day seven fishermen who had been clamming
at Back River the morning Jenny and Sash were there came
in town to be quizzed by Dr. Vanderslice. Reporters kept a close
watch on Dr. Vanderslice's office and who was coming and going.
Some of the clammers posed for photographers, their white shirt-
sleeves rolled up, their faces tanned and burned by the wind and
sun—leather-like by exposure to the elements. They were from
Messick, a little fishing village in York County. They talked freely
of their suspicions of what had happened near the lonely Back
River Light, of hearing screams and seeing Mrs. Kane in the water
only up to her waist, until the fishermen were rounded up by the
police and warned not to do any more talking to the reporters. The
clammers were kept under close watch after that.

When the coroner came out of his office, he approached the
men from the press saying he wouldn't be able to tell them much
at this time. Then shaking his head, suggesting an emotional depth
he felt, he said, "The more I hear, it's not looking good for the
professor. You can be assured I have taken down in longhand every
word that was said here today. I want my record to be absolutely
correct," he told the reporters. "And so I see to it, that it is correct,

by making it myself. We will get to the bottom of this. Then we'll be able to tell you more."

"Dr. Vanderslice," the reporters crowded in on him, "were there marks on the body that would indicate strangulation?"

"The livid color of her face when examined immediately after her death indicated she might have been strangled, but later inquiry among the hospital staff showed this condition did not prevail until after resuscitation methods had been used."

"Dr. Vanderslice," a reporter questioned, "we understand the professor told a different story from what you've heard from these men today."

"The man closest to the scene has partly substantiated Dr. Kane's version of the affair," the doctor answered. "He admitted hearing Dr. Kane scream for help after reaching the beach and said the accused professor apparently picked the body up and dropped it down several times, which is a substantiation of Dr. Kane's claim that he made an effort at resuscitation."

"You said yesterday, Dr. Vanderslice, that there was no evidence of violence on the body of Mrs. Kane and that her lungs were filled with water."

"Gentlemen, please. We don't know what we're going to find. There may be another woman involved. There are some missing letters. Once we find them, they should clear up a lot of loose ends. There is no question Mrs. Kane drowned, but whether it was accidental, or homicidal, is to be determined."

"The letters you mentioned, Doctor… Can you tell us who wrote them?"

"We don't have that information at this time," Dr. Vanderslice said. "We believe her initials are B. H. D."

Mr. Cock, the Commonwealth's Attorney, added to the coroner's remarks, "We know that Kane and his wife have been virtually estranged all summer." The disheveled, lanky attorney waved his long arms to disperse the gathered reporters.

The Arrest Warrant for Elisha Kent Kane

"You mean, they were separated?" an excited reporter asked as Mr. Cock urged the coroner to pass through them.

"I am not prepared to say what caused the estrangement."

"Who is the attorney representing Professor Kane?"

"Professor Kane has not retained counsel," Mr. Cock answered. "Nor has he asked to see an attorney. That's all we can give you now, gentlemen. Thank you."

Someone spotted Hop Graham coming out of the building. "Mr. Graham, do you think your brother-in-law killed your sister?"

"If Jenny ever went into the water deep enough to drown, she was carried there," Hop responded.

"Then you…"

"Gentlemen, please," Sheriff Bickford Curtis said. "Let Mr. Graham by. The investigation is under way. You gentlemen will be informed of any new developments." The name Curtis was synonymous with law-enforcement on the Peninsula. Henry Curtis was Hampton's Chief of Police, and Leslie Curtis was an officer. Elvans Curtis was a deputy sheriff for Elizabeth City County, and Chriss Curtis was a sergeant at the Newport News city jail. Perhaps Chriss was the only one who wouldn't take part in the case of the woman drowned at Back River Light.

The headlines told of a search for missing letters. "The missing letters are believed to be the capstone to the web which the York, Warwick and Elizabeth City County police are endeavoring to weave around the thirty-seven year old professor held in jail here on a charge of murder." The news stories hinted at a love affair of the young educator. The B.H.D., it was suggested, possibly was a Betty Dodd.

Investigators were searching Elisha's apartment in Knoxville for any evidence that might shed some light on things. The university officials refused to allow a search of Sash's office on the campus.

The Enterprising Counselors

*B*efore the newspapers had printed any story about the drowning death of Jenny Kane, Frank Kearny, an ambitious young attorney, got wind of the news.

"This is it," he told his friend, Percy Carmel. "I tell you, this is the case we've been waiting for. A University of Tennessee professor was arrested for the drowning death of his wife. At the Back River Lighthouse. Her family's from Hilton Village. The couple went swimming, and then he brings her back to Dixie... dead."

Percy shifted his cigar to one side of his mouth and said something about "the poor drowned girl," but Frank paid no attention to this.

"The girl's brother went to the coroner and said something wasn't right. He doesn't believe the story his brother-in-law told. So here's the deal. I'll get the family to hire me to help the prosecution. You go after the professor. It's going to be a big case, my friend. This will be the making of our careers."

"Why do I have the feeling you haven't told me everything you know?"

"I haven't. I must be true to my clients."

"You haven't any clients..."

"But I will," Frank insisted. "Now, you show up at the preliminary hearing and make yourself known to the Kane fellow. This is going to get big. He's from a wealthy Pennsylvania family. Name your fee. They will want the best defender, and you're it."

Percy and Frank shared a home on Mallory Street in Phoebus, a small community across the Queen Street Bridge from Hampton. Before leaving to go to law school at the University of Virginia, the boys had noted that one of the attributes of being a Hampton lawyer was they would partake heartily of alcoholic beverages. The elder men had enjoyed the "spirits" long before the days of prohibition, and this was a law that didn't apply to them.

But Frank and Percy, anxious to have their own law practices in the city, weren't so confident they would get through law school, or have that same privilege, even after graduating, to ignore the law. They agreed to set a new precedent at UVA—they would not partake. The two graduated from the Charlottesville law school and had been practicing law, though in separate offices, for about ten years. They had talked of going head-to-head in the courtroom. They were looking for "a good, clean fight."

Percy and Frank were as dissimilar as Bud Fisher's comic strip characters, Mutt and Jeff. Percy was slim and of average height. Frank passed two hundred pounds and kept going. Percy was Jewish. Frank was Irish Catholic. Percy was a dandy dresser, always looking dapper. Frank was the big sport's fan—big enough to be good at most any sport himself, though as Percy said, not a "speed merchant" on the track.

There was a special camaraderie that existed within the legal community in Hampton. Soon Percy and Frank, neither afraid of hard work, were welcomed into the fold. Frank readily went to work defending bootleggers against the Federal revenuers. Percy joined the office of C. Vernon Spratley, one of Hampton's most respected lawyers. After a few years, Spratley became the Circuit Court Judge of Elizabeth City County. Recently Percy's younger brother, Macy, had joined him in his law practice. Percy was pleased at the thought of Macy having an opportunity to get in on this murder case. Yes, he and Macy would be at the preliminary hearing. He would present himself to Professor Kane.

The *Daily Press* reported the arrest of Elisha Kent Kane Sunday afternoon at Hilton Village, only a short while after Mrs. Kane was buried. "Dr. Kane at first declared that his arrest was an 'outrage' and told the officers he didn't know what it was all about. He, however, quietly submitted and was placed in a waiting automobile and brought to Hampton by the three officers."

The paper said the warrant charging him with murder was read to Dr. Kane. Magistrate Joseph Dixon had sworn out the warrant after hearing testimony from fishermen who were clamming near the Back River Lighthouse the morning of Jenny's death and upon reports that letters were in existence tending to show that a New York woman may have been involved.

By Tuesday afternoon, Percy and Macy Carmel had a client with a murder charge against him. Elisha Kane was sitting in the Hampton jail awaiting the coroner to complete his investigation, so Percy could apply for bail… if they didn't release him. Frank and his brother, Ross Kearney, joined in the prosecution by assisting the Commonwealth's Attorney, Roland Cock. Newspapermen, photographers and curious people crowded around the jail hoping to get a look at the professor who had been arrested for drowning his wife.

The arrest attracted nationwide attention. Sash's association with a half dozen institutions of learning and his prominent Pennsylvania family lured out-of-town correspondents to the small town of Hampton, Virginia. "Never before in its more than three-hundred and twenty years of existence has the oldest continuous English-speaking settlement in America occupied such prominence in national print as it has since the arrest last Sunday of Elisha Kent Kane." The local *Daily Press* told of the Kane family's ancestry going back to eleventh century England. The professor was clearly from noble stock.

It was rumored the Graham family, portrayed as of lesser means than Jenny's husband's family, had retained Harry Smith, Jr., a criminal attorney from Richmond, to help the prosecution. Percy read from a brief article in the paper to Macy, "It says when Mr. Smith was asked if he had been retained by the family of the deceased, he told reporters, 'Nothing has been determined, and, accordingly, there is nothing for me to say.' But it looks, brother, like we're up against the big boys, and they're about to turn up the heat.

"I asked Winston Read to help us out," Percy continued. "He knows this fellow Smith. The coroner has spilled enough to the press to keep an army of us busy. The *Daily Press* has shown an interest in the man's accomplishments, but who is paying attention to that when this 'Mysterious Woman' is what they want to read about?"

"The story about the blacksnake whips in Sash's automobile was corrected," Macy said, "but probably no one read the correction. And it makes sense that a man in the National Reserves had a revolver with him, when he just came in from Ft. Bragg. But telling the public he had the gun only makes them think of the professor as some diabolical brute."

"Right," Percy agreed. "I need you to talk to Kane about this library book they found. It's going to take some fast talking to explain why Sash had this manual for drowning someone in his car."

"Is that what it's about?"

"What?"

"The book, *An American Tragedy.*"

"It's about a man drowning a girl he had made pregnant so he could marry another. It was banned in Boston. The author based it on a true story," Percy said.

"Did the man get away with it?" Macy asked.

"No, he died in the electric chair, which is what could happen to our client if we don't do some pretty fancy footwork here," Percy said. "Like, for instance, one of the fishermen told reporters Sash had rushed Jenny's body ashore before he could render any assistance. In the testimony they first gave Dr. Vanderslice, none of the fisherman

"This is it. This is the case we've been waiting for."

— *Frank Kearney*

"Brother, it looks like we're up against the big boys, and they're about to turn up the heat."

— *Percy Carmel*

said they made any effort to help the girl. I'm inclined to think the man realized people would wonder why he hadn't helped Jenny, so he just said he couldn't catch up with Sash. Sash said he was shouting to the fishermen. He wanted them to help him."

"You believe Sash is innocent?" Macy asked his brother.

"I do. And you do, too. Once you sign on with a client, it's imperative that you believe in him. You tell your client to tell you everything and, no matter what he tells you, you believe him," Percy answered. "If your client says he did it, you believe that, too. You go before the jury and say anything, short of lying, to get him off, because you're supposed to do all you can to get him off."

"I've heard this speech before, Percy. Just answer my question."

"Fortunately in this case, Sash says he didn't drown his wife. He doesn't impress me as being cagey. He's an odd son-of-a-bitch, which makes him seem suspicious to the folks around here. But it's our job to convince the jury not to convict a man because he's a strange duck. The man sits in his hot cell, in nothing but his underwear, grading his students' papers or working on that translation like he hasn't a care about what's happening to him. He couldn't kill anybody. His mind is lost in some romantic literature—too distracted from reality for him to be able to kill anybody."

Frank Kearney's confidence in the case against Sash was just as intense. The two friends argued before the court concerning bail. After the professor had spent a week in the Hampton jail, Frank boldly demanded that Judge Spratley allow the State to continue to hold Sash without bail. Percy stood up protesting, "Not granting bail would be against the laws of the State, Your Honor. Even in capital cases where 'very peculiar circumstances are present,' the law states a reasonable bail must be set."

"I believe counsel is correct, Mr. Kearney. It remains now to fix the proper amount."

The Commonwealth's Attorney stood up, "What would be sufficient bail for an ordinary prisoner would not be sufficient bail for the scion of a prominent and wealthy Pennsylvania family," Mr. Cock said. "In view of the fact that this man had his bags packed and was ready to leave this community when we arrested him on a murder warrant last Sunday, it seems to me that the Court should fix a sum large enough to ensure his return here.

"Your Honor," the prosecutor continued, "The suspicion of guilt against him is very strong indeed. The Coroner, after a most painstaking investigation, has given an unequivocal verdict of murder. I think that bail for one-hundred thousand dollars would be reasonable." Murmurs throughout the courtroom caused the judge to bring down his gavel.

"Your Honor," Percy leaped to his feet, "Such an amount is outrageous and prohibitive. It would be folly to admit a man bail and then fix a figure that would be tantamount to refusing him bail. The Commonwealth's Attorney has made very determined and persistent efforts to keep this man locked up," Percy said. "I don't know what he hopes to gain by it, but the laws of this State insure a man his freedom in bail in a case like this, and my client is entitled to bail at a reasonable figure. I will not suggest a figure. I leave that to the sound discretion of the Court."

"The court sees your point, Mr. Carmel. Therefore an amount of fifteen-thousand dollars is the bail set by this court."

Even that was a huge amount that would require additional time to raise. Sash would spend one more night in jail while funds were transferred from a Philadelphia bank. The energetic man had begun to show signs of the drudgery of his confinement.

Percy spoke with reporters after the hearing. He pointed out the jail had been an ill-adapted place for conferences between the accused and his attorneys. "We are pleased with Judge Spratley's decision. My client, who is used to clean linen, will be pleased to see the light of day tomorrow."

"Does your client still claim he's innocent?"

"He does," Percy answered. "Gentlemen, I have complete confidence in Professor Kane's innocence and our plans for his defense will be whipped into shape immediately."

Percy laughed as he read one journalist's account of the hearing: "Frank A. Kearney, slow-footed but nimble-witted two-hundred and fifty pound attorney, demanded... the professor be held without bail."

The Pennsylvania Entourage

*A*t his client's request, Percy had brought Sash his papers to work on in his cell. Sash said he wanted to finish his project on *The Book of Good Love*. The small space in which he was confined soon looked like the office of an absent-minded professor, totally oblivious to his surroundings.

Jenny was buried in the cemetery of the historic St. John's Church. The jail was next to the old graveyard. At night, when things got quiet—when the sounds of the curious public had ceased for the day and even the reporters had gone home—when Sash no longer had to make his thoughts block out the voices outside, he was a prisoner. The cell that at least offered him solitude during the day, at night would not release him to visit Jenny's grave, so close and yet so far away.

It was on one of these lonely nights Sash decided upon the inscription he would have on the headstone of his wife's grave. He wouldn't order the words "Loving Wife and Daughter" as he had first thought. The inscription would be in Italian, a quote from Dante's "Inferno":

JENNY G. KANE

1898—1931

Nessun maggior dolore

Quel ricordarsi del Tempo felice

Nella miseria

In the work of Dante, the characters Paola and Francesca are telling Dante the tragic story of their lives. "There is no greater grief than to recall a happy time gone by in days of misery." Sash requested butterflies be carved in the upper corners of the gravestone above the inscription.

Dr. Evan O'Neill Kane learned of his son's arrest from the newspapers. He was a patient in his own hospital in Kane at the time. His left hand was being treated for blood poisoning. He had received the infection while operating on a patient. Immediately, he telegrammed Percy. "The man took out his own appendix," Percy told Macy, "and he's likely to operate on me if I don't get his son out of this mess."

"I got the impression from our client that he and his dad weren't very close."

"Well, Dr. Kane's telegram reads like Daddy is already on his way."

Reporters met the plane when Sash's father first arrived in Hampton. Somehow, he convinced them he was deaf and spoke Scandinavian. He managed to get past them without answering any questions. The father of this "giant," as Sash had been called, was a small man. He wore his suit jacket over his left shoulder, his sleeve flapping loosely, as his bandaged hand could not fit through the sleeve.

Sash's father was accompanied by his nephew, Mr. Kent Kane, Jr., of Bradford, Pennsylvania. The nephew, a first cousin of the accused, was a prominent attorney in his home state and would assist with the defense.

Earlier that same day, Mr. Francis Fisher Kane arrived from Philadelphia. That Mr. Kane, a first cousin of Sash's father, had served as the United States District Attorney in the City of Philadelphia under President Wilson.

One journalist said of the capacity crowd attending the hearing, "If I could get the concession, I could make a tidy sum charging

Gravestone at St. John's Cemetery

admission to the Kane hearing—in spite of the depression."
Another reported: "Hampton knocked off crab-packing, oyster-shucking and other gainful occupations and, with a large part of the population of the rest of the Peninsula, massed on the Elizabeth City County Courthouse in full expectancy of a snappy murder trial."

The crowd was described as largely female, "many of them young and pretty and obviously enjoying their first experience in a courthouse." One such spectator was quoted as being "tickled pink" to be there. Men too thought they had experienced the grandest of all thrills when Elisha Kane came to court with "the other woman" on his arm. There had been an overnight rumor the now infamous Betty Dahl would arrive in time to appear in court on behalf of the accused.

The word spread quickly throughout the crowd that "Betty is here!" Like the crowd at a circus marveling at the sight of Siamese twins, they stretched their necks to see. "She is pretty, the hussy!"

But excitement soon became disappointment when the truth circulated amongst the crowd that the woman was not "Betty" after all. The woman they had seen with Sash was his cousin's wife.

Summer temperatures lingered into September, and the mercury had risen well over ninety degrees even before the hearing was to begin. The old courthouse was jammed almost to the point of suffocation. Local soda fountains did a thriving business.

It was Kent Kane who addressed the reporters on behalf of the family after the hearing. "My cousin is more of a scholar than I had imagined," he told them. "He is determined to divert his mind with work upon this translation, which has occupied much of his time the last five years. Of course, he has no desire to have it published posthumously, but it is the one thing he wishes to finish at the present moment. Even if he is executed, he is going to finish this translation."

"Has his father visited him? Has Elisha been speaking with his attorneys?"

"Yes, to both questions. My cousin made a real effort to look sharp for his father. Evan Kane is seventy-one. Elisha put on a coat and arranged his hair when his father visited him, so that his father would not worry about his appearance. To keep his father from feeling bad, he acted as if he hadn't a care in the world. As to talking with his lawyers, Lashy has relayed to us in great detail what happened at the Back River lighthouse."

"Lashy?" The reporters echoed the name.

"Excuse me, gentlemen. The family has called him 'Lashy' since he was a boy."

Kent made light of the evidence that Elisha Kane was about to leave town when arrested. Kent pointed out the accused man had no reason to stay. "His wife's people were not friendly towards him. He wanted to go home to Kent to be with his family in his time of grief." Of the "Betty" letter, Kent only said he had not seen such a letter.

"Tell us about the Kane family, Mr. Kane."

"I don't know where the Commonwealth's Attorney ever got the idea, as he stated in court just now, that the Kanes are a wealthy family," the attorney answered. "They are not. Members of the Kane family have always gone in more for fame than for wealth." The newsmen chuckled at that remark and turned to Francis Kane.

"Mr. Kane, do you intend to take part in your cousin's defense?"

"I am quite satisfied with the way in which the Carmel brothers are handling the case."

Percy and Kent approached the members of the *Daily Press* staff and requested the paper run a story asking the women, said to have spoken with Sash at Grandview that day, to communicate with them. "We are anxious to have them support the evidence that Dr. Kane appealed to them for a doctor."

That evening, the impassioned patriarch of the Kane family and his cousin, Francis, appeared before Dr. Vanderslice. The testimony of the two occupied nearly two hours. They were allowed to visit the accused briefly afterwards. They returned to their hotel exhausted and with no reason to believe the coroner had wavered in his opinion.

The crowds were well aware of the presence of the Kane family on the little peninsula. Talk of how the wealthy Pennsylvania family was going to pay the professor's way out of his predicament buzzed throughout the courtroom onto the streets of Hampton and up the road to Hilton Village. When Elisha, finally, was permitted to leave the courthouse, he was not alone. His father and his cousins were with him. Perhaps the show of strength of this prominent family from out-of-state did more to prejudice the local people against Sash. That he was a college professor, tall, handsomely tanned and from a good family, had only seemed to make for rumors that he thought he was too good for his wife and her humble family. There was, however, a growing group of young women who would have been willing to pay a concessionaire any price for a seat in the courtroom when Sash would next have to appear.

More encouraging to the accused were the several hundred telegrams and letters from his colleagues, students and friends from other sections of the country, expressing sympathy and confidence in his innocence. Several of these Sash carried in his coat pocket as they consolingly reminded him of the respect many outside of this area had for him.

He was still wearing the light gray coat he was wearing when they arrested him. His white shirt was spotless, but his days in jail left him looking rumpled, and his unruly hair was resistant to combing. He wore a modest blue cravat. For days he suffered the stares and whispers of people who found entertainment in the process of his indictment for the murder of his wife. Every blink of his eye, every glance towards a window, the way he held his hands, the slightest expression of despair or relief was fair game for the reporters. The kind words he held in his pocket were his lifeline.

"Unqualified confidence in and sympathy with you in your present bereavement." (signed by ten of his former co-workers)

"We offer our sincere sympathy in your present bereavement and wish to express our faith in your innocence of the charge brought against you." (signed The Ritts Family, Knoxville, Tennessee)

Gripping the telegrams in his pocket, Sash faced the reporters as he left the jail. "First of all, I want to thank you for your courteous treatment. I'm glad to get out, although they treated me very courteously while I was confined. It was my first experience in jail. It was interesting, but not pleasant."

"What do you say…"

Before the question was completed, Sash continued with his prepared message. "I could look out into the cemetery where my wife is buried. I clung to those bars, thinking of the happy times we had together. That was one of the most torturing experiences in jail."

"Will you stay here?" someone asked.

"I have no intention of leaving. I will fight this murder charge to the finish. And I will be found innocent."

"Contrary to what has been said in the court, my son is a member of the Presbyterian Church."

— *Evan O'Neil Kane*

"Do you expect to see the Grahams, Dr. Kane?"

"May I say that I understand that Mrs. Graham has been upset by her recent illness. Of course, I have been unable to see her. As for the actions of Mr. Graham and his son, W.H. Graham, I think they will be fully explained later."

Percy and Kent were pleased with the way Elisha presented himself to the reporters. Then they got the latest newspapers. An article Sash had written for the Knoxville *News Sentinel* the year before was now being republished in all the papers.

KANE WRITES OF HIMSELF

He'd titled this tongue-in-cheek piece, "Autobiography Told with Frank Dishonesty." Now his words came back to be scrutinized by the public. "I never tell the truth, when a lie can be more entertaining," he wrote. "In my write-up—as in my life—we shall not be able to separate truth from fiction.

"I am modest, quiet, dignified, staid and devout," Sash wrote. "I lived a normal boyhood; that is to say I disobeyed my parents on all occasions, fought, lied, stole, swore, played hooky and ran away from home. As I grew older, I continued this wholesome existence. I was expelled from five colleges and two universities... I hiked and biked all over Europe picking up whatever languages seemed easy, and they all seemed to come that way. I banged about the world drinking deep of whatever experience had to offer... Some time back, I got married and sobered up—marriage does that you know...

"Now, if a man has made a failure in everything," he concluded, "he can always still get by at teaching or preaching. As I wanted to be honest, I took up teaching. Unlike some of my colleagues, I like my students immensely."

"I think he comes across like a regular fellow with a good sense of humor—most affable," Macy said. "You don't think people will take everything he said seriously, do you?"

"Most people will find it amusing in the way he meant it to be," Percy said.

"But the people who want to think he's guilty," Kent said, "will read it like a confession."

"We're getting plenty of newspaper coverage," Percy said. "Frances gave a statement to the *Philadelphia Inquirer.* Allow me to read...

> A bitter little Virginia town is determined to find Elisha Kent Kane guilty of the murder of his wife.
>
> It is stacking the cards against the "stranger"—bringing to bear against him all the forces of clannishness of an isolated, prejudiced community.
>
> In his cell, the university teacher cries occasionally, horrified at the charge, and broken over the loss of his wife. From the strictly legal standpoint, there isn't enough evidence to convict Professor Kane. And from the standpoint of my personal investigation, Kane did not kill his wife; he loved her too much to harm her.
>
> I knew the prosecutor had some letters, and I asked Lashy about them, and about the woman who wrote them. I think he told me the truth about everything.

Percy looked up from the newspaper at his colleagues, "They printed what Sash told him—every word of it......

> I had an affair that I am ashamed of now. There is a woman I met while traveling, and we went around together. It was a mistake such as many men have made. She wrote me letters, and Jenny discovered some of them. Naturally, she was heartsick, and she spoke to me. We talked the thing over at great length. I did everything I could to make amends. Finally the matter was settled, and I thought all the letters were burned. That was two years ago, and since that time I have never seen that girl. If she sent me any letters later, God knows I didn't get them. If they are accusing me because of things said in a letter I never received, what can I say?
>
> The affair was ended. Jenny and I had become reconciled. It's absolutely ridiculous to think that I could have drowned my wife because of this woman.

I have tried to tell them exactly what happened on the day Jenny drowned; but to tell the truth, it happened so suddenly that there are some things I don't even remember.

We went swimming at the spot in the bay where we have been going for years. I swam out into the deep water... I heard her call for help. She seemed to moan, and I saw her slip into deep water and sink. I swam to her side so fast that I was almost exhausted when I reached her. She was under water, and I had to dive to get her.

Then I put one hand under her chin and swam with her to the shore. She was limp.

Finally, I got her to the beach and then I collapsed myself. I had called for help as I swam and was terribly sick, as I often am when excited.

I carried her to the car, where our dog was sitting and barking. I rushed her to the hospital. There I became ill again from the excitement.

They gave her a hypodermic and tried to save her with a pulmotor. I begged them to get another doctor...

"Frances didn't leave anything out," Percy summarized. "I think the people of Philadelphia would have Sash released immediately."

"I wonder what the locals here will think if they read the part about a bitter little Virginia town and a prejudiced community," said Macy.

"He goes on to say they should have made a quiet investigation first, and requested Sash remain in town," Percy had been reading ahead. "He mentions the awful stigma which has been fixed on an innocent man because of the way they've handled the case. Then he says there was no reason for the coroner's inquest to have been secret. He says it made things look mysterious and bad."

I honestly feel the authorities here have been proceeding, not with an open mind, but with a feeling they must find my cousin guilty of murder—Percy read again.

My cousin's father-in-law is a country squire—he is scheduled for election as Justice of the Peace again at the next election—and he has a certain amount of political influence. He was certainly always prejudiced against Lashy. It has been very easy to arouse feelings against him.

"The story Sash told Francis," Macy asked, "was it different from what he told Dr. Vanderslice?"

"It wasn't verbatim," Kent answered. "If you ever hear an accused give the exact words of what happened over again, you can be pretty sure it's fabrication."

"Repeat that," Percy said.

"When a client tells me his side of things twice and uses the very same words, I usually find he is lying."

"And you've proven your point well, Counselor. When I asked him to repeat what he said, Macy, Kent said almost the same thing but in a different way. When a person experiences something traumatic, the shock of what is happening is so unbelievable he can't explain it to himself. The prosecution wants to take issue with the distance Sash said he swam. Could any of us answer such a question under similar circumstances? Here Sash says she was limp. Before he said she pulled him down with her. Both statements can be true—first she struggled against him—then she went limp and he was able to pull her to the shore."

"Or perhaps he was anticipating having to struggle with her, but it really didn't happen," said Macy. "He just got confused, like a child who wandered off and got lost. He was so worried about the scolding his mother would give him, he later remembered she did; but she says she was so glad to see him, she couldn't."

"I believe I remember what you're talking about, Counselor," Percy said smiling at his brother.

"I talked with Sash about the book they found in his car," Macy said. "He told me he'd just seen the movie version of the story at a theater in Knoxville. He checked the book out because he wondered how it differed from the movie."

"Okay," Percy said. "Just to be prepared for anything the Commonwealth wants to say, I want you to check out the book and the movie. Let's find out how dissimilar the story is from this situation."

"So far as the book is concerned, there's not a lot of similarity once you get beyond the fact that you have a man and a woman in water and the woman drowns," said Macy.

"The man is uneducated. He gets one girl pregnant and falls in love with another one. The sweet, but pathetic, pregnant girl is pressuring him to marry her. The voluptuous, wealthy girl is offering him the world on a silver platter. Finally he gets the one he knocked up in a boat—she stands up—the boat dumps them both in the lake—she can't swim—he swims to the shore and takes off like nothing happened."

"Did my cousin say why he was so interested in this story?" Kent asked.

"The author of the book has filed suit against the Hollywood producers because he doesn't feel the movie told the story he wrote," Macy explained. "Sash says he wanted to see how Dreiser—that's the author—showed a man might be pressured into doing something that wasn't in his nature to do."

"Yes, Lashy would want to do that," Sash's cousin agreed. "It's unfortunate that he had this particular book when they searched his car. Most of what he reads is written in a foreign language and has some mystical meaning no one else would be able to decipher. Like this thing he's translating. It's a classic, but they won't sell many copies."

"Tell me about Sash and his father," said Percy. "Is his father really going to stick beside him in this?"

"Lashy wasn't as wild as what he suggested in his autobiography they republished, but he was not an easy child for Cousin Evan. Lashy's mother died of pneumonia, I think, when he was an infant. For years his grandmother raised him. Then Cousin Evan remarried. Lashy's stepmother seemed to think Lashy was a difficult child. I think Cousin Evan issued a few ultimatums to Lashy—you know the kind—'This is the last time,' etcetera. Lashy, or rather 'Sash' as they call him here, has five half-brothers, but he was the only child of Cousin Evan's first wife. It always seemed to me Sash thought his father didn't love him like the others, and I thought he loved Sash more.

"But you asked if I think Cousin Evan will stand by his son," Kent said. "Don't be fooled because he went home right away. He had to get that hand well. He doesn't like to fight with one hand tied up. He'll be back with both fists swinging."

The Script Tease

*N*ewspaper headlines declared:

    EFFORTS TO LOCATE A COMELY BRUNETTE IN NEW YORK

Or they called her "the mystery woman, the other woman or just Betty. Where was the woman who had possibly plotted the drowning death of Jenny Kane? B.H.D.? First the authorities said they were looking for a Betty Dodd. Then they said the initials were those of Betty Harris Dahl of New York City. Deputy Sheriff Thomas Curtis of Elizabeth City County traveled to New York, Philadelphia "and elsewhere" on a fruitless search for Betty Dahl. She was wanted in connection with the drowning of Mrs. Jenny Kane. Meanwhile the newspapers alluded to a possible secret rendezvous—Professor Kane, Kent Kane and the merry divorcee, an ex-stewardess aboard sundry ocean liners. Dr. Vanderslice said her letters would incriminate the professor, but the State hadn't located the woman, or the letters.

Finally Commonwealth's Attorney Cock and Dr. Vanderslice released a letter from "Betty". It started "Sashy Dear" and included a couple of lines that the prosecution lifted from the letter to suggest Elisha's guilt.

The communication was addressed to Mr. E.K. Kane, Box 4141, University of Tennessee, Knoxville, Tennessee. It bore the return address, 150 East Riverside Drive, New York.

Newspapers printed the letter in full:

On Board S.S. America,

September 1, 1931.

Sashy Dear,

Have you read in the news that the U.S. Lines are near on the rocks, that this ship is to be laid up this trip? This throws about 500 out of work on her including me, but I am not going over my bridge with worry until I need to because I may get a break still with the company. And really no one knows anything definitely until we arrive tomorrow.

In any event, it gave me opportunity to see Berlin four days and fly to Paris in an 18-passenger Fokker, which consumes six and one-half hours. Had eight days in Paris. I do think it is the most expensive city I have ever visited as a tourist. I am very, very keen on Hamburg, the night life is as gay as Paris, but much more perverted. I saw moonlight life in Paris (can you imagine that) but I am told it is much bolder and gayer than Paris.

There are numerous times, Sashy, when I wondered if you and I ever get leisure to do some of the old world places together—the good and the bad. Which reminds me of the enclosure, it fits you so admirably. Do you still have any dreams of my ever being a part of your life? If you ever get rich, would you take me to the unusual, and would we do the unusual? I can't understand how come she stayed at home a year. Do you still intend to stick it?

And how about the book? Truly are you devoting your time to it strictly but surely—is the dedication still to "B.H.D."?

What are you doing with your days this summer, Sashy? I really don't believe I've let a day go by without thought of you. We were once so close and still feel close to you. If you were not now at home you could easily drive to Washington and take a bus there. I like the buses.

I would adore seeing Washington under your tutelage, but I suppose this cannot be.

Gee, Sashy, where do you go? Is there a heaven for good days? A hell for bad ones? Purgatory for merely dull? Seven of them passing every week. To where? And why?

Sashy, I have meant to ask you so often, how is the colitis? Are you nervous? How is your work?

Will you take this letter and answer all my questions—soon and by airmail?

Did you mean it you would give me a cigarette case? You may be sure I would hold on to it this time. Anyway, it shows you keep your promise.

Were you in camp this summer? Jerome, my brother, has been selected as assistant coach and executive officer of the rifle team at Perry. Before these orders from Washington, he had just been sent to Knox in charge of a demonstration team. He won the presidential medal last year, sharp-shooting at Perry.

My sister drove to California this summer. Told her to look you up if she passed your way. Have you read any interesting books? You know the kind I mean.

Well, dear, this is a long letter from Betty, who still holds you very, very dear to her heart.

The *Daily Press* ran a sub-head, "'Do You Still Have Any Dreams of My Ever Being Part of Your Life?' New York Woman Asks." The entire text of the letter followed an opening paragraph that pointed out that "this was the first tangible proof… of the existence of correspondence about which rumor had woven an imaginative tale."

"Cock claims Betty's letter encouraged you to get rid of Jenny," Percy told Sash.

"Betty would never suggest such a thing," Sash replied. "Besides, I never saw it."

"That's right," Percy agreed. "The letter was forwarded after you left Knoxville and it was intercepted by the Grahams, having been delivered to their home. Were there any other letters from Betty the prosecution might have?"

"As I said, I corresponded with this woman for awhile until Jenny found some of the letters. I haven't written, or heard from her in a long time. If they have other letters, I haven't seen them. Yes, I had an affair with this woman years ago, but I'd made things right with Jenny."

"They don't have any other letters," the attorney was thinking aloud. "Cock wanted to make you look guilty. It's safe to assume this is the best … or rather, worst he had to release to the press."

"I know the letter won't sound proper to some people," Sash said, "but that's Betty's way of speaking."

"Listen to what the letter says…she's been in Berlin, Hamburg and Paris," Macy noted. "She wants to know what you've been doing. Did you go to summer camp? Anyone can tell she hasn't heard from you in some time."

"Don't underestimate the damage that's been done," Winston Read cautioned the others. "The media is going to have a ball with lines like 'take me to the unusual and do the unusual.' We need to find this woman before the prosecution does."

"Betty's mother lives in Mt. Holly, New Jersey. Perhaps she can help you locate Betty," Sash told them. "She's a widow."

A friend of Betty Dahl spoke with reporters announcing the woman was engaged to be married to an Englishman she met on the liner *Leviathan*. She talked of Betty's life. She said Betty had eloped with Harry Dahl when they were very young, and the marriage had not worked out. They had a child, but it only lived to be a few months old. Betty met Sash while she was working in a canteen during the war. "That was before he was married, or even knew his wife."

The friend also described Betty "as different from anyone I ever knew. A lot of people don't understand her straightforward and honest viewpoint. There must be a reasonable and perfectly decent explanation of a letter she is said to have written to the professor."

Mrs. Dahl's sister-in-law spoke with reporters hoping to convince people Betty's alleged "love missives" were not "affectionate." She told them, "They were written only with the frankness of a woman who is writing a friend she has known for a long time."

When the press found Betty's mother, she told reporters she had been instructed by defense lawyers not to make any statements. She told them her daughter was in Philadelphia and would go to Virginia to testify in the professor's defense. In fact, her daughter's fiancé would also be willing to testify for Sash.

A Philadelphia paper reported the mysterious Betty was hiding there. At home in Philly, Francis Kane was asked if he had interviewed Betty. He "refused to deny" that he had. The paper also said it was possible Sash and Kent had a secret meeting in Philadelphia with the woman. Authorities in Hampton believed the professor and his cousin were holding a conference with the missing woman in either Washington or Baltimore.

In front of the Elizabeth City County Courthouse, Kent Kane answered questions of reporters, "The defense has no fear of that letter. The accused has never seen it."

"Will Mrs. Dahl testify for the professor?" the reporters asked.

"The defense will probably call Betty Dahl to the stand if the State is permitted to introduce the letters she is alleged to have written."

The Whispering Spectators

*T*he University of Tennessee wasn't the only place cutting salaries. The Stock Market's crash in October of 1929 had cast its shadow on the whole country. Still the small communities of Tidewater Virginia, with populations of shipbuilders and fishermen, had not been so abruptly marked by the stigma of the depression. Federal spending at military bases in the area helped to delay its effects. And in Hampton, the news of the murder trial offered a diversion from the financial news. Everyone became a detective.

So many people went to see the place where Jenny drowned that no one could see the lovely secluded place it had been. The little cone-shaped Back River Lighthouse sitting on a mound of rocks, the shallow waters creating a soft melody of waves breaking against them and the flat beach meeting the wide expanse of "Grandview," were looked at as a murder scene. No one visualized the couple, happy to be back together, playing in the surf. Many felt they could hear Jenny's screams. Few thought about her husband, frantic to help her.

"Why did he bring her so far away from other people if not to kill her?"

"She wouldn't have drowned in this shallow water unless he was holding her down."

"The fishermen saw him do it. They saw him holding her down."

There was a pilgrimage of people visiting the grave of the lovely young woman who drowned down by the Back River Light… probably at the hands of a "wife slayer." Most of them eyed the Italian words inscribed on her stone and wondered at their meaning.

Once Sash was released on bail, he would go to his wife's grave that was just outside the walls of the old jail. Kent warned his cousin of the crowds of curious mourners. The men tried to slip in the graveyard at a very early hour to avoid the onlookers. Nowhere on the peninsula would the tall, very distinguishable, professor be able to go unnoticed and, least of all, at the church cemetery. As Sash knelt in front of the grave he could hear whisperings of people who were gathering around to watch him… until he read the verse upon the stone. Sash heard the voice of his wife, "Pappy. My Pappy! You're here."

He would have collapsed upon the grave, had he not been told Hop Graham accused him of theatrical displays of grief. He stiffened his body to hold himself upright. Kent stepped up next to Sash, offering himself as a leaning post. Neither of them spoke. Kent heard the streetcar passing on Queen Street. He heard the church bells chime. The foghorns of ships wailed as they navigated through the early morning mist on the Chesapeake Bay. The crowd occasionally shifted as new members joined to watch every move of the accused husband. A train whistle announced its arrival at the station. Two crows cawed in conversation. Kent wanted to think the birds, at least, were cawing about the gathering of catty spectators and not meaning to be cawing at Sash.

When the church bells began to chime again, Kent quietly suggested it was time to go.

"The tombstone is lovely, Lashy. It says it so beautifully." Kent took the hat from his cousin's hands and placed it on the man's head, and helped steady him.

They left the cemetery and the idle chat of those who had been observing them took on renewed enthusiasm.

"Here's an article in the *Washington Herald*," Percy told the team of lawyers gathered in his second-floor office of the Bank of Hampton Building. "The reporter says they expect a record attendance when Magistrate Dixon calls the Kane case. He says,

Never before in recent times has the Virginia Peninsula been so stirred over a court case...

"Never before in recent times. That's what it says."

The Doleful Lad

"*W*hen was the last time Hampton had a big murder trial?" Macy asked.

"It was in 1920," Percy answered. "Before I got out of law school. But I followed the case. A woman named Mittie Jestep Cumming shot and killed her ex-husband."

"She had a little boy, didn't she?" Winston Read asked.

"Yes, and her defense attorney, Richard Byrd, didn't need to do anything but make little Kenneth Cumming visible to the jury. Everyday they'd take the child to see his mom in the jail. And Byrd made good on the devotion between the mother and her child.

"Mittie went looking for Samuel Cumming with a loaded revolver. She shot the man several times… in front of witnesses. Cumming was a brilliant lawyer, but he supposedly used his knowledge of the law and his lawyer friends to take advantage of Mittie. Byrd defended her showing Cumming treated her dreadfully. The teary-eyed little eight-year-old lad appeared in the courtroom. They let him sit by his mother during the trial—his arms about her neck. There wasn't a man in there who could send his mother away from him.

"Well, not a man other than Roland Cock. He was the acting Commonwealth's Attorney in the case. He said, though her ex-husband didn't give her as much money as she thought she needed, she didn't have the right to kill the man."

"Wasn't there something about a pre-nuptial agreement?" Mr. Read asked.

"You're right," Percy said. "I think Cumming married her so the boy would have a name, but Mittie was supposed to divorce him after the child was born. Only she didn't want to leave. Something like that."

"She was found not guilty on what basis?" Macy asked.

"Temporary insanity. Cock argued it wasn't a temporary thing when she had threatened him. She borrowed a gun saying she needed it for protection, loaded the gun and went after her ex-husband.

"The courtroom was filled and overflowing into the corridors. No matter what Cock said there was no sympathy for the deceased. Mittie got on the stand and cried, 'I loved him too much to kill him!' It took the jury less than four minutes to find her not guilty."

"Do you think the jury made the wrong decision?" Macy asked.

"Do you?" Percy bounced the question back at his younger brother.

"Well, Cock had all the legal arguments, but the jury system worked for Mittie. It was decided on the evidence her husband had persecuted her. I think they were right."

The Faithful Shepherd

*K*ent walked in the law office. The others turned towards him as if expecting a report. After a few minutes of silence he said, "I left Lashy in his room at the Chamberlin. He was sick— very near a nervous breakdown. We drove to Hilton earlier to see Mr. Graham about getting his dog back."

"I hadn't heard about this," said Mr. Read. "What kind of dog is it?"

"Hop Graham refused to let Lashy—Sash, have his dog yesterday," Kent explained. "He claims Sash abuses the dog. We went out there today to tell them I will institute a suit to obtain custody of the dog. Hobo is a German Shepherd. His pedigree name is Vuga. The father of this dog was Strongheart, the movie star. Jenny and Sash, both, have been very devoted to him. He went everywhere with them. Sash put a canopy in the rumble seat of his car. That's where Hobo always rides. He wants his dog. I'm going to see he gets it. Sash is all to pieces."

"I remember Strongheart," Macy said with such enthusiasm one would have thought they were well acquainted.

Everyone paused to see what Macy was going to say.

"Well, I saw him in person. He went on a train ride across country. He had a car to himself and the train made whistle stops all along so fans could get to see Strongheart. He seemed bigger in life than on the screen. Most of the cities they passed through gave Strongheart a "key to the city" to hang around his neck."

Turning back to Kent, Mr. Read asked, "Do we need to have a doctor in to see your cousin?"

"I don't think so. I think he's suffering from a let down after the six days of incarceration and everything he's had to go through since his arrest. Strange, but I think Sash is having trouble adjusting to being out of jail. The experience of being in jail was so bizarre, it didn't fit with anything else, and he could think it wasn't happening. He'd like nothing more than to be able to sit in the cemetery where Jenny is buried and weep his heart out. But he can't do that with all the people there to observe him."

"It's going to be impossible for him to stay here if he's indicted," Mr. Read said. "Even a notorious, but short fisherman could blend in around here, but the lanky Pennsylvanian will not have a private moment."

"I'd like to think he won't be indicted," said Kent. "They haven't got a case against him."

"Mrs. Graham is feeling better, and it looks like she'll be their star witness." Mr. Reed said.

"Lashy can't believe she's turned against him," Kent said. "I wish we could talk with her."

"I think it would be good to get your cousin out of town for a few days," Percy said. "Sash said he wanted to go to Knoxville to arrange for his classes to continue until this mess is over. Could you drive out with him?"

"Yes. That's what we'll do. There's nothing he can do here now—nothing new he can tell you. It will be good for him to go out to the campus and see some friendly faces."

"If we could really pick a jury of his peers, they wouldn't just acquit him, they'd vote him into office," Mr. Read said. "Your cousin—what was that the newspaper said? 'Youthful-figured, but grizzled-haired university professor'—is well thought of on the college campuses."

"Funny thing, he's always been a nonconformist. The family didn't understand where he was coming from when we were boys," Kent said. "He's turned out to be an unorthodox professor, yet he gets hundreds of letters from people—students and faculty—who believe in him, expressing their respect and sympathy."

"The news people seem to have taken a liking to Sash," Macy said. "He plays a game with them. They ask him about the case and he tells them about the book he's translating. But he does it so well, you know he's so pleasant in his manner, I can tell they like him."

"It's a good thing they like him," Kent said. "Imagine what they could do to him if they didn't."

"Kent, you make points for our side when you speak with the press," Mr. Read said. "You always give them something they can quote and you give it to them with sincerity and spunk that makes for good copy. That piece you did for the International News Service should give people something to think about."

"Can we find twelve jurors around here who haven't been persuaded already that Sash is a wealthy, highbrowed, philandering wife-murderer?" Kent asked. "That Dr. Vanderslice didn't want to hear anything we had to say."

"Dr. Vanderslice is well loved by the people of this area," Percy said. "When we had the flu epidemic back in '18, that man made house calls all night long all over the Peninsula. His bedside manner is a little gruff, but people have a great deal of respect for him. He's been known to offer his services free of charge."

"What do you think of him?" Kent asked Percy.

"I think he's wrong on this one. But he's a good man. Perhaps he's not as sharp as he once was."

"It seems to me the man has come to think of himself as judge and jury," Kent said.

"Yes," Percy said, "I can see why you think so. You might be right."

The Capitol Barrister

*T*he letters Jenny wrote Elisha during the summer were found in the Kane's apartment in Knoxville. A small portion of one was published in the *Daily Press*.

> You are so sweet and good to me. I appreciate everything you do and want to be forever with you and, honey, its raining and I can't swim and it makes me sick. I love, love, love you. When are you coming to me?

Of the search of the apartment the newspaper article said the officers found nothing of incriminating nature—just endearing letters from his wife signed "Babe" with several X's (to send kisses).

Marshall and A.L. Johnson of the Grandview area appeared before Dr. Vanderslice. They saw the professor and Jenny when the professor was driving away from the beach. They had seen the couple at Grandview numerous times, and they always went to the lower end of the resort to swim, and they always had their dog with them. This time, they said Dr. Kane was driving rapidly in the direction of Hampton, continually blowing his horn, and running over the rough roads without slowing down. They did see him stop below the pavilion and speak to three women who were in a blue sedan.

"Misses" Emily and Mollie Robelen, two ladies whom Sash had seen at Grandview and appealed to for help came forward to substantiate the professor's story on the last day of Dr. Vanderslice's inquest. The sisters were from Richmond. Still, as Kent had said, the doctor didn't seem to hear anything that might reverse his earlier decision.

Meanwhile, Sash's remark that he could look out from his jail cell into the cemetery where Jenny was buried was received with criticism. "There is no way that man could see the grave of his wife when he was in jail." No, he couldn't. He could see the cemetery, but not her grave. The headline, which read, "Kane Tortured By Looking At Grave Of Wife From Jail," was the work of an overly zealous reporter. It was not a direct quote from the accused.

"The Grahams retained Harry Smith," Macy told his brother. This time he read to Percy,

Hiram Smith, of Richmond, a noted criminal lawyer, has been retained by ...

dah, dah, dah.

W. C. Graham, the father of the dead woman, said last night that Smith will come to Hampton Tuesday to confer with Commonwealth's Attorney Roland Cock and Frank Kearney, who have conducted the prosecution to this point.

Mr. Graham said that his son, W.H. Graham, of Phoebus, visited the noted criminal lawyer at his office in Richmond yesterday...

"dah, dah, dah. It says the Grahams reiterated that they believe Sash is guilty," Macy said...

"We have retained Mr. Smith in the interest of proper representation of the family in the case. We will cooperate with the Commonwealth in seeing that justice is done."

"Then it says something about Smith and the Beattie case two decades ago. Anybody know the particulars of that one?" Macy asked.

"You should," Percy answered. "Certainly you studied that case in law school."

"I can't believe you will say that Elisha Kane
III, is the only person who has told the truth."

— *Harry Smith*

"The man, Henry Beattie, Jr., told authorities he and his wife were stopped on the road by a man carrying a gun," Mr. Read said.

"Y-y-yes, he said the man shot his wife," Macy recalled. "He moved towards the man, and there was this blast, and his wife fell forward. He said he struggled with the man and was knocked down having been hit across the nose. The man dropped the gun and ran. At least, that's what Beattie said.

"The police investigation couldn't find any evidence there had been anyone on the road, and so they got suspicious of Beattie. Beattie's cousin got on the stand and told that Beattie had killed his wife. But the defense tried to show the cousin might have been jealous of Beattie.

"The State had the owner of a hardware store tell he sold shells to Beattie, and a dairyman told of seeing Beattie on the road earlier which, the State said, gave Beattie the opportunity to hide a gun behind a stump for later use.

"Then the State brought in a surprise witness, Beulah something," Macy said.

"Beulah Binford," Mr. Read offered.

"Yes, they brought in Beulah Binford," Macy continued. "She told of a relationship with the defendant that started when she was just a child. When she was only fifteen, she had Beattie's baby. The child had died, and it was the child's death certificate that lead the State to Beulah.

"No matter what was said, Henry Beattie remained cool and cocky. He posed for photographers with a smile on his face and his straw hat propped on his knee. He sat in the courtroom reading the comics while someone was testifying about his wife's blood on the highway. It was said he did himself in with this attitude. When he testified, he told his story without emotion.

"In spite of all the elegant words his defense attorneys had for their closing remarks, Henry didn't have a friend on the jury. When Harry Smith stood in front of the jury, he proclaimed someone had suggested 'the deeds of Henry VIII of England formed the greatest blot on the escutcheon of England. And I say that this crime of Henry Beattie has formed the greatest blot on the escutcheon of Virginia.' It was beautiful, the way he said that," Macy concluded, standing up and delivering the remarks as an attorney would in court.

"It was well said, and you've quoted it well," Percy said with a big smile. "But that was from Louis Wendenburg's remarks. He was working for the Commonwealth. Smith was defense counsel. He had a brilliant closing, but, as you said, the smiling defendant hanged himself."

"Harry Smith was the Commonwealth's Attorney of Richmond for two terms. Since then he has served as defense counsel in most of the important criminal cases all across the state," Mr. Read said. "It's not whether you win or lose. It's how you play the game. Hiram Smith knows how to play the game."

Hop begrudgingly brought the dog to Percy for its return to Sash before a suit was filed. The Grahams told reporters Sash had been cruel to his pet, but when Percy brought the dog to Sash, he saw contradictory evidence. The dog, who was a witness to what had happened at Grandview, affirmed the affection he had for the man. *If only Hobo could testify, he could clear Sash of the charges*, Percy thought.

It was cleared with the local authorities for Kent to accompany Sash to Knoxville to see that his fall classes would continue in his absence. Kent, Sash and Hobo drove to Knoxville. Kent felt like an impostor sitting in Jenny's place. If things had been as they were supposed to be, Jenny would have ridden back to Knoxville sitting where Kent was sitting—Sash entertaining her with some naughty rhyme from the archpriest's *Book of Good Love*. Their debts finally paid off, they would be anticipating easier times ahead. Hobo would be content to be going home again.

Sash sang no merry rhymes. There would be no returning to things as they had been. Even Hobo was listless, his sad eyes conveying the loss he felt.

Colleagues and students, most of them teary-eyed, greeted the professor and expressed their astonishment that anyone could think he would have killed his beloved Jenny. Many volunteered to come to Hampton to testify in his behalf. Sash offered to resign, but the president of the university wouldn't hear of it. "Don't worry about anything, Elisha," Dr. Morgan said. "The truth will be found, and you will come back to us."

The cousins returned to Hampton in time to appear at the preliminary hearing before the magistrate, Joseph Dixon, on the last day of September. The magistrate who had been the Mayor of Phoebus for several terms, for the last several years had been a justice of the peace in the Chesapeake district.

The Commonwealth's witnesses included the coroner, members of the Graham family, a neighbor of the Grahams, their minister and several of the fishermen from Messick, Virginia. Dr. Vanderslice had made public a thirty-page typewritten report of the inquest sessions. The details of his report were printed in the newspapers. Now Dr. Vanderslice and Roland Cock selected which of those testimonies were to be repeated before the magistrate. The courtroom was crowded with women who laughed and chatted at intervals despite repeated warnings from the justice. They even applauded the fine points of victory of both the prosecution and the defense indiscriminately.

The Meticulous Coroner

*D*r. Vanderslice was the first witness called. Kent questioned the doctor. "Am I to understand you gave a verdict of accidental death after you examined the body and then changed it to homicide after members of the Graham family suggested murder… before going into physical facts?"

The coroner answered that he changed his opinion after talking to the fishermen.

"Did you examine the body to determine positively if Mrs. Kane drowned?" Kent asked.

"I only examined the body to see if she received an injury to her head," Dr. Vanderslice said, "also for bruises on her body."

"After foul play was suggested, why didn't you hold a post-mortem?" the attorney asked.

The doctor answered, "I thought I had seen enough to satisfy me that death was due to drowning."

"Doctor, at the time it was suggested to you there had been foul play, the body was still where it could have been examined?"

"Yes, sir, but it had been embalmed."

"It had been embalmed at that time? Did you consult the undertaker who had prepared the body?" Kent asked.

"No, sir. I did not. I think the family told me."

"Don't you think it would be of importance in a case of this type to find out whether or not the undertaker observed anything upon the body?"

The doctor shrugged. "Hind thoughts are better than fore thoughts, Judge. It would have been wiser."

"Even as a forethought, would not you think it would be wiser to consult the undertaker as to the physical condition than to ask the members of the family?"

"Well," Dr. Vanderslice answered, "I usually make my opinions for myself, sir, and rarely ask the assistance of the undertaker."

Finally Kent asked, "You changed that death certificate to homicidal drowning without making any further examination of the body, is that correct?"

"Not on the suggestion of the family," the doctor replied, "but on the statement of these men, and not on the suggestion of the family did I change my opinion. The suggestion of the family required that I should have investigated the matter. I—of course, there are many things we might regret. I would like very much to have done a postmortem—that is the reason I am coroner. Your Honor," he turned to speak directly to the justice, "knows we have very little opportunity to do postmortems, in private practice, and I am particularly interested in that kind of work, and would very much like to do postmortems on every case where it is possible to do so consistently. I have made a rule to do it."

"Well, Doctor," Kent asked, "did anybody at this time object to your performing a postmortem examination of the body?"

"No, sir, not in the least."

"Well, why didn't you hold a postmortem examination?"

"I was of the opinion drowning was the cause of death."

Kent continued questioning the coroner who seemed to be getting more and more confused.

"Dr. Vanderslice, at the time Hop Graham consulted you, you say he told you there were certain letters which indicated a motive?"

"Yes, sir."

"Where are those letters?" Kent demanded.

"One of them is in the hands of the sheriff, to be produced when desired. The other letters, he told—I understood he told me in the beginning his mother had them, but that he was not so sure about it; and he told me when he returned the second time he was of the opinion the letters had been destroyed—that his mother was in such condition that it was very difficult to determine that fact, but he was of the opinion the letters had absolutely been destroyed."

"Mr. Hop Graham was of the opinion?"

"Yes, sir."

"What did you ask him about other than letters?"

"I don't know, possibly I asked him to look and make a further effort to find them."

"Did Hop Graham say he had ever read those letters himself?" Kent asked.

"I am not so sure he said he had read all the letters," the witness answered. "I am quite sure he said he had read some of the letters."

"Did he say he had read any other letters besides the one that was actually given, which he showed you at the inquest?"

"I am not sure he did. Anyway, he told me some of the things that were in the letters, and I am not so sure whether I asked him whether he had read them individually or not or whether his mother, who had them in her possession at the time, had told him the contents of them, I can't be absolutely sure. I think Mr. Graham can tell you that," the doctor suggested.

"Did he tell you at that time anything else about the letters?" Kent asked.

"Now, let me get this straight. As I remember it, if I remember rightly, that is 1929, Mr. Kane—Major Kane, perhaps, he was then as is now, a major in the reserve corps, and was in camp at Fayetteville, North Carolina, at which time there was a woman who was with him who was—who seems to have been, I understood to be a nurse—he said that the family understood that she was a nurse.

They didn't know all the details. That following this, when the Kanes returned to Knoxville, certain letters were received at home, re-enveloped and addressed from Chapel Hill, North Carolina, to Mr. Kane at Knoxville, Tennessee, and that these were opened by his—by Mrs. Kane. These letters were the kind—that was in the fall of 1929—the letters that were not produced. The letter that was produced was September first."

"Doctor," Kent asked, "According to the best of your knowledge then, from this hearsay testimony of Mr. Hop Graham, these letters were opened by Mrs. Kane at Knoxville?"

"That is my information, but I have no personal knowledge of that."

"How did Hop get to know the contents of the letters?"

"He said these letters were kept by Mrs. Kane and afterwards turned over to her mother when she went to Knoxville to see them," Dr. Vanderslice answered. "I think he said that Mrs. Kane kept them and after that visit destroyed them."

"I didn't get that quite clearly," Kent said. "Who did you say destroyed them?"

The addled doctor tried to get his words to come out right. "She didn't say. I say they were destroyed. I didn't say who destroyed them, and I would not like to say whether it was Mrs. Graham, or Mrs. Kane, or anyone else destroyed them."

"Did you have a letter at the hearing dated September first?" Kent asked.

"Yes, sir."

"Which I believe was signed 'B. H. D.'?"

"Yes, sir—no, sir, it was signed 'Betty.'"

"Was that the letter which Hop Graham referred to as having been received at Hilton Village?"

"Yes, sir."

"Who received that letter?"

"I could not tell you that, sir. I understood his wife received it, I understood Mrs. Kane received it, I understood," the doctor

"I want my record to be absolutely correct.
And I'll see to it, that it is correct, my making
it myself."

— *Dr. George Vanderslice*

repeated himself. "I understood that she received it, but I would not like to say just how much. I understood she received it and opened it."

"Upon what basis do you say you understood that she received it?" Kent asked.

"Well, sir," Dr. Vanderslice said, "I am quite sure that Mr. Graham told me that, but that I have not made a matter of record in my memory."

"Doctor, did Mrs. Graham tell you at the hearing that was conducted at the house that she had shown this letter to her son but not to her daughter?"

"Let's see if I catch that."

"Did Mrs. Graham," Kent prompted the witness, "testify before you at the inquest that she, that is Mrs. Graham, Mrs. Kane's mother..."

"Yes, sir."

"Had shown the letter to her son but not to her daughter?"

"You mean the last letter?"

"Yes," Kent said. "The last letter?"

"May I refresh my memory, your honor?"

Justice Dixon answered that he could.

"I have not a copy of it."

The Commonwealth's Attorney offered him one, "Here is a copy made in your office."

Dr. Vanderslice examined the copy of the notes he had first taken in longhand and then typed before presenting it to the court.

"Take all the time you want, doctor," Kent said. "Whether she made the statement 'I showed the letter to my son but not to my daughter'?"

"I wonder if I can ask the clerk to send me up the original copy?" the coroner asked.

"Here is a certified copy," Percy offered the copy to the doctor.

"I understand, but I want my own handwriting."

Mr. Smith approached the witness, "Doctor, do you want your statements here to go in the record?"

"No, I was just talking to Mr. Carmel. I was just talking to him."
Then finding a place in the document, "I expect this is it."

"Have you finished your examination, Doctor?" Kent asked.

"I asked for that paper. I think the punctuation may be different.
I am not so sure. If you will recall, I took these papers in longhand,
and under the circumstances, which were not..."

Again the attorney for the State from Richmond spoke, "I am
just making the observation, if you intend for the stenographer to
get this you ought to talk loud enough."

"Well, I don't want it," Dr. Vanderslice said as he accepted
other documents and examined them.

"Did you find it?" Kent asked.

"Yes, I found the place," the doctor answered. "I am not so sure
about that, but I put her statement down as carefully as she told it.
If she was referring to that particular letter and nothing else... but
at this moment I cannot recall absolutely. The witness can be
produced and she can clear that matter up herself."

"Doctor, those words, 'I showed the letter to my son and not to
my daughter,' are, however, in your handwriting?" Kent asked.

"Yes, sir, and it is my opinion, but I am not sure which letter
that was. I am not so sure that was intended for letters or letter.
This was written in longhand and taken down under very distressing
and difficult circumstances. I am not a stenographic reporter."

"Doctor, let me refresh your memory on another point you
heretofore testified to:

That Mrs. Kane had received those letters, she had received them
and turned them over to her mother. So there would be no sense
showing them to her, as Mrs. Kane received those in Knoxville."

"Yes, sir, and showed them to her mother."

"Yes, sir," Kent said.

"My vague recollection is, that I have probably made a slip in
my—in my assumption, I mean in copying it, and that in the haste
of copying it in longhand, as a person speaks, I should have turned
it exactly around. That the letter was shown to her daughter and

not to her son, because… she feared trouble between her son and Dr. Kane. That is my recollection." Satisfied with his deduction the witness stiffened his body and shook his head.

But Mr. Kane was not satisfied. "I object to that."

Mr. Smith stood up, "I object. As you insisted on getting that answer, I don't see how you can object to it."

"I object," Kent answered, "to his statement about his notes being wrong. If that is wrong, all the rest of them are wrong." There was a stir of laughter in the courtroom.

The witness addressed the justice. "The coroner attempts to make a careful reproduction of the statements made. Your Honor must know we are all fallible, and sometimes in the haste of writing we twist words absolutely unintentional. My impressions are I tried to give you this was simply an error in copying rapidly under the stress of a great deal of difficulty, the nervous stress of this mother who had a great deal of difficulty in telling these things, and who was emotional and very much distressed, as you must know. That in doing it, I meant to write and at the same time, momentarily, put down the same story, and the words are reversed. 'I told my daughter and not my son,' because I understood her to say, she feared trouble between the family. In fact, I understood them to say that some members of the family wanted to go to Knoxville and take the matter up in a more violent manner."

"All right, Doctor," Kent said, "if she then stated to you and your recollection being better than your notes, that she showed the letter to her daughter and not to her son, how does it come that Hop Graham, who came to you, knew the contents of the letter?"

"That was afterwards."

"But the mother stated she didn't show Hop Graham the letter and Hop Graham was the first one to come to you, is that right?"

"Well now," the doctor said, "you are mixing the two letters. Personally, I got it from the notes, because I don't remember—I don't remember they were—these notes—now you are trying to get a record of facts, and I told you I feared I made an error in copying off her statement, so that I left out enough to show exactly what you are referring to. And I am sorry. I ask not to be held down to that statement, when the witness can be produced and can state what she did say."

"And I am equally sorry," Kent said.

"The witness can testify as to what he remembers about it," the justice spoke to Kent.

"Yes, sir, he can testify to what he remembers. Now, there has been ample opportunity, sir, for the witness to change her testimony perhaps, when the purpose of the coroner's inquest is to determine what it is at the time, before they have time to think it over."

"Your Honor," the coroner turned to the bench, "If I understand the ruling of the Supreme Court, no actual evidence produced at the coroner's inquest can be produced in court. The evidence is taken by the coroner when the witness is present and the defendant is not, and is not represented by counsel. The witness cannot be cross-examined, and consequently the evidence cannot be produced in court. Now the witness can be produced, and if they have testified in such a manner, that testimony can be contradicted by the coroner."

"I think you are perfectly correct, Doctor," Justice Dixon answered.

"I have a copy of the coroner's report," Kent persisted, "and it shows in the witness's handwriting, that statement."

"Well," the doctor answered, "I assume I put down the statement, as nearly as possible, that was made by the mother. If I did make an error…"

Justice Dixon prompted, "You did it unintentionally?"

"I did it unintentionally."

The Decisive Justice

*T*he one Graham family member Sash thought would never testify against him was the prosecution's star witness. Jenny's mother appeared deathly pale, her hands and face jerking with nervousness. Frank Kearney questioned her. She said Jenny had acted strangely the morning of her death. Mrs. Graham, thinking her daughter didn't want to go to the beach with Sash, told Jenny she didn't have to go. "But she went anyway—I saw her face through the window—and she looked at me as much as to say: 'Oh, Mother, keep me here! I don't want to go.'"

Then the frail, little woman sobbed and sagged in the witness chair. "They went, and my darling daughter never came back alive!" Mrs. Graham gave way to hysterics.

The mother was excused. There was no opportunity for cross-examination. The professor stood at sympathetic attention as Mrs. Graham stumbled past him.

The Commonwealth called eleven witnesses to tell of screams heard and two people struggling in the water, of the defendant making conflicting statements and that "help was at hand but not called for." The defense attorneys had not summoned witnesses to testify, but cross-examined each of the State's witnesses again and again. Dramatic scenes of strenuous legal quibbling brought outbursts of partisan applause from the courtroom while Justice Dixon, hammering away with his gavel tried to bring order to the court.

At the end of the day, Roland Cock told the court there was a reasonable probability of guilt and asked that the defendant be held for the Grand Jury.

Winston Read said the new statute provided that "not probable but just and sufficient cause of guilt" must be proven before a case could be sent to the Grand Jury. He told the court the testimony "showed as much probability of innocence as guilt." Mr. Read asked the court, in reference to help not being called for, "If your wife were ill, would you call a clammer, or a doctor? Would you take her hurriedly to the hospital as the defendant did? It means nothing but injustice to put this man on trial on the evidence presented here. We have not heard one iota of fact to suggest this man did anything wrong, and we ask for dismissal of the case."

Applause from about half of those in the courtroom broke out spontaneously as the defense counsel finished his appeal. Justice Dixon rapped for order, "I'll have no more of that applause, and all other expressions of hilarity must cease."

Frank Kearney stood up. "This man," Frank pointed at the suave-looking defendant, "has given conflicting testimony, and there are sufficient suspicious circumstances for charging him with the crime. You do not have to have direct evidence to prove a man guilty of murder. The circumstances here indicate that murder has been committed and that there is sufficient evidence for holding the accused for the Grand Jury."

Again applause broke out in the courtroom. The justice rapped for order. He cast a glance about the courtroom and without any emotion in his voice, said, "Held for the action of the Grand Jury."

The professor stood, strode over with his hand outstretched to the old criminal lawyer from Richmond and remarked with his characteristically morbid humor: "It would be an honor and a pleasure to be sent to the chair by a man like you."

"I'll have no more of that applause, and
all other expressions of hilarity must cease."
— *Justice Joseph Dixon*

To the reporters outside of the courtroom, Sash said, "It is good that I have been indicted. Dismissal, at this time, would not be vindication."

The Adoring Dames

*A*ll the king's men and all the king's horses couldn't find "Betty." There was little doubt the defense knew where she was, but they weren't telling. "It's plain this woman has something to hide," Roland Cock told the press. "She certainly doesn't want to talk to us."

On December 8th, the day Elisha Kane's trial for the murder of his wife began, Betty Harris Dahl came out of hiding. In a copyrighted article, Mrs. Dahl said she wanted to get the facts straight. For three months she had tried to avoid the public, because she didn't trust the "overzealous" prosecuting attorney not to twist what she'd say to his purposes.

Newspapers ran her written and copyrighted deposition for two days. She spoke of Sash as "the most brilliant tender-hearted man" and called it "ridiculous" that he should be accused of such a crime. She hoped by telling her story—"hurling herself at the gossips"—an innocent man might go free.

In the first part of the article, Betty told of her life up to the time she met Elisha. She said that after the death of her child she was working at Ft. Knox as a secretary. Then she said she attended a dance at the base and asked Sash to dance with her. He was not married at the time. She was processing for a divorce. They danced, they talked, they became good friends. They had "a very precious romance."

In the second part of her story, Betty told of Sash getting transferred, and due to a misunderstanding they ended their relationship. Betty didn't see Sash again for ten years. One lonely day she decided to write him to see what had happened to him. She said they then exchanged letters about once a month, Sash telling her he had married "a lovely girl."

A couple of years ago, Betty and Sash met in New York when Sash had a business engagement. She said they spent the major part of the day at the Museum of Natural History, and Sash talked a lot about Jenny. She said they agreed to correspond—"our past love and present interest and friendship for each other warranted some contact," but she never expected to see him again.

Betty said Sash's letters to her often spoke of Jenny. He told her of Jenny nursing him through a bout of the flu. He said that, unfortunately, Jenny came down with the virus also.

Betty's explanation for the "unusual" comments she made in the letter that had been printed in newspapers across the country was that she was referring to Elisha's love of traveling "odd roads and by-ways." She said friends told her she had a "romantic complex" in writing letters, which might explain her phrasing.

Betty denied having written words that would suggest anyone ever "get rid of anybody" and said she knew nothing of Jenny Kane's death until she read of it in the newspapers. She closed saying that she was willing to go to Hampton to testify if the defense called her.

The day of the trial rumors abounded. Many anticipated the appearance of "Betty." Roland Cock said he hoped she would come as the State still held that the accused's involvement with Mrs. Dahl led him to murder his wife. It wasn't known if the State had more "Betty" letters to introduce.

Sash had spent some time in Kane, Pennsylvania, at his father's home. A week before the trial was to begin, he'd returned

"My friends say I have a romantic complex in writing letters."

— *Betty Harris Dahl*

to Virginia and was staying at the Warwick Hotel in Newport News where he was holding daily conferences with his attorneys. Sash's father and brother would also be staying at the Warwick during the trial. It was understood that Mr. Harry Smith would be staying at the Chamberlin at Old Point.

Nearly a hundred witnesses were summoned by the Commonwealth and the defense to give testimony. Stating Elisha drowned his wife by holding her under water until death ensued, the Commonwealth of Virginia was asking for the death penalty on a first-degree murder charge. The indictment alleged premeditated and deliberate murder.

Roland Cock said he had no "sensations" to reveal in the trial. The presentation of the State's side would require only one day. Mr. Smith of Richmond would be sitting at the Commonwealth's table with the Kearney brothers and Roland Cock. They admitted the case was based on circumstantial evidence: Sash desired to get rid of his wife because he was infatuated with another woman. No witness was found who actually saw Jenny drown. "In a few hours following his wife's death," Mr. Cock told the jury, "this man talked to at least a half dozen people and told as many stories."

A number of former Commonwealth witnesses, including three fishermen, were summoned by the defense to testify. Although the defense didn't summon them, several people from Tennessee, including Dr. Dewey Peters, Professor Stratton Buck and Mr. and Mrs. Lee Ragsdale, were all coming to testify on the professor's behalf. Dr. E.A. Abernethy would drive from Chapel Hill, North Carolina, to testify for the defense. The Robelen sisters were summoned to come from Richmond. A swimming instructor at the Chamberlin would be testifying for the defense, and a Mrs. Kimball of Hilton Village. Dr. Evan Kane would be sitting at the table with his son and the defense team. They intended to show the jury Jenny may have suffered an attack when she fell in the water, and Sash did everything he could to save her.

Percy Carmel and his friend, Frank Kearney, who shared a home, were each still confidently eager to fight this battle in court. Each felt their side would win. Each respected the other team of lawyers and prepared themselves for rigorous conflict. When in the courtroom, one represented the Commonwealth and one represented the defendant.

Perhaps when they said, "My distinguished colleague," speaking of the other, they were more sincere than some lawyers. They each expected the other to give their very best in this fight.

The telegraph companies installed special wires in the county police room in the rear of the courthouse for the army of news people who would be covering the trial. The news would be reported to every part of the United States and many foreign countries. Judge Spratley provided the men and women of the news services, "the scribes" as he called them, a section of the courtroom to the right of the bench and within a few feet of the attorneys' tables.

The courtroom that seated three hundred could not accommodate the crowds of people who wanted to attend. People crowded around courtroom windows trying to see. Those not lucky enough to get to a window waited outside to hear reports of what was happening.

Reporters said of the crowds, "They are mostly women—scores of them, thrilled by Elisha Kane's romantic mien and figure." Certainly there were those and they thought the man was too nice looking to have done what he was accused of. There were others who thought he was too nice looking... not to have done what he was accused of. To some he was a gentleman and a scholar. To some he was an egotistical presumptuous womanizer. One had to get a pass to get into the courtroom, and no one dared leave for fear of losing a seat. Some brought their lunches. Mr. Fertitta of the Langley Confectionery across the street, being a smart businessman, hustled lunches to others who didn't want to give up their places. Many people of the Peninsula waited at home to read of it in the *Daily Press* or the *Times Herald*, but almost everyone was keeping up with, and had an opinion to express about, what was happening in the murder trial of the professor from Pennsylvania—the wealthy one who drove around in his roadster—the man who was cheating on his wife.

"Gentlemen, this case must be completed
this week. If necessary, I will have to call a
night session."

— Judge C. Vernon Spratley

The Honorable Spratley

*F*ew in the courtroom knew better what to expect from Judge C. Vernon Spratley than Percy Carmel. Percy's first law office was with Spratley's practice. Others might think Percy would have an edge on the prosecutors. But Percy knew better. The judge would be able to decipher his every move. Judge Spratley would view his performance in court as a piano teacher would watch a student's recital. Percy wouldn't want to hit the wrong chord. It would require everything he had to please the court.

Still, Percy did know his mentor well and could read him. He knew Spratley would maintain order in his courtroom, while at the same time obliging the requests of the newsmen. He knew the judge was savoring the publicity this case had drawn—ballyhoo and all. But the judge wouldn't deem a man guilty because he was a maverick. Quite the contrary. All the strange twist and innuendo would be most gratifying to Spratley.

The Twelve Men, Tried and True

*A*s the trial had received tumultuous publicity, Judge Spratley asked for a "venire" of sixty men. In late November, summons were issued by Sheriff Curtis to sixty men in Hampton, Phoebus and Elizabeth City County. They were to appear in the Circuit Court on Tuesday morning, December eighth, the date of the opening of the Kane case.

Additional guards were placed at strategic points about the courthouse to keep the crowds from getting out of hand. Crowds came to hear the attorneys battle over the admissibility of testimony. The jousting of knights in King Arthur's day could have been no more exciting.

Court was called to order, and "The Honorable C. Vernon Spratley" was announced by the bailiff.

More than a dozen of those called veniremen admitted to having formed an opinion, and they were excused. A couple of men said they were opposed to the death penalty. One man said he was opposed to circumstantial evidence. Sixteen men were selected after as many were excused. Then the attorneys on both sides were allowed to eliminate two of the sixteen.

The twelve agreeable to both sides included a bank cashier, an auditor, a bookkeeper and a real estate man; a foreman, a draftsman and an official from the Newport News Shipyard; two auto salesmen, the owner of a furniture co-op, a music dealer and a retired merchant. The somber group took seats in the jury box. The jury was sworn to "well and truly try and true deliverance make in the case of the State of Virginia against Elisha Kent Kane, III."

Sash tried to maintain a calm composure before these men who would decide his fate. Deputy Clerk Giddings turned towards Sash and commanded that he stand while the indictment was read to him.

The Elizabeth City County Courthouse
on King Street in Downtown Hampton

The Commonwealth's Repertoire

*D*r. Vanderslice was the State's first witness. In his testimony he said he'd been called to the hospital to view the body. He arrived a little after the noon hour. He told of talking with Dr. Kane and Kane told him that his wife had dived from a rock and was overcome. He said the professor told him he tried to save his wife and attempted first aid before rushing her to the hospital.

Percy cross-examined the coroner. Vanderslice said he'd found no bruises on the body and hadn't done an autopsy as he was lacking any reason for suspecting foul play.

The Commonwealth called Rev. J. D. Hozier of the Hilton Methodist Church. Rev. Hozier was a long-time friend of the Grahams. Mr. Graham would fill the pulpit at Hilton when Rev. Hozier was away. The minister said Dr. Kane had told him Jenny called out to him, and he rushed to her aid. He hadn't said anything about any fishermen nearby, nor had he said anything about trying to revive his wife.

The third witness, Mrs. Wilbur Hudgins, Hop Graham's mother-in-law, said Sash had told her he was teaching Jenny to dive. He said fishermen were about a quarter of a mile out, and he couldn't get their assistance. Mrs. Hudgins also testified that two years ago she had found Jenny crying because Sash was talking about a divorce because of another woman.

Then Mrs. Hudgins' sister, Mrs. Marguerite Knowles, supported her testimony and offered she had never seen Jenny Graham get her feet wet at the beach, much less attempt to swim. She said she had been to Grandview with Jenny many times.

The State had the deputy sheriff who had arrested Sash take the stand. Bickford Curtis said Dr. Kane seemed surprised on being arrested, but that he'd had no conversation with Sash at the time. On depositing his valuables at the jail office, jewelry belonging to his wife had been found in a handkerchief in one of Dr. Kane's pockets.

The deputy sheriff said he questioned Dr. Kane about his being infatuated with another woman. The man had admitted being with another woman at the base and again in Atlantic City.

Curtis said he then asked if this woman had written to him suggesting that he murder his wife and quoted Sash as answering, "My God, no; nothing like that ever happened."

Next, W.H. Pride, a Hilton schoolteacher and friend of the Grahams, told of asking Sash to tell him what had happened down at the Back River Light. He said Sash told him Jenny had called out to watch her and then began screaming. He went to her assistance and, at the same time, called to the fishermen for help. Jenny went down twice before he reached her.

Mr. Girard Chambers, the county engineer, was asked to explain with the aid of a chart of the Back River, measurements he had made of the area. Percy cross-examined Mr. Chambers, who then explained the currents run stronger above than below the lighthouse, because of obstructions. Probable depths of three to five feet could be encountered.

Mr. Richard Johnson, the keeper of the Point of Breakers lighthouse, gave a technical discussion of the depths of the water around the lighthouse. He stated that at low tide the water was about three feet in front, a little deeper on the north and not so deep on the south. "The tide," he said, "rises and falls about three feet. On a clear day there is practically no current."

The Commonwealth called Mr. Clyde Saunders, a friend of the Grahams, and he told the court what Sash had told him. He added Sash told him he had had a course in first aid.

One of the sisters from Richmond told of Sash asking them to phone "the hospital and tell them my wife is dying." Mrs. Hazel Wells, the nurse at Dixie, told of his arriving at the hospital with Jenny in a red bathing suit and a cap strapped tightly around her neck.

The Peace Keeper

*B*efore any testimonies were given, Mr. W.C. Graham had been named as the State's chief witness. A reporter described him as he appeared on the witness stand: "W.C. Graham, the dead woman's justice father, six-foot and spare, dressed in black, with a low stiff collar and black tie, a huge old-fashioned moustache, horn-rimmed glasses and a cowlick sticking from his crown."

Jenny's father stated that he was employed by the land company in Newport News and was a Justice of the Peace in Hilton Village. He told that before he left for work the day of the tragedy he found Mrs. Graham in conversation with Jenny and Sash in the kitchen. "Jenny appeared unusually sad," he said.

"Mr. Graham," Roland Cock asked, "what can you tell us of the relationship between your daughter and her husband?"

"When they were out together, they were apparently happy," the father answered, "but when they were in their room together alone, there was constant abuse heaped upon Mrs. Kane. He would curse and abuse her in a way I would not treat a dumb brute"

"Why did your daughter stay with Dr. Kane, being as he treated her so badly?"

"She loved him, notwithstanding his harsh treatment," Mr. Graham explained. "Dr. Kane knew Jenny would die before she would leave him. She knew her husband's disposition, and she did not jump on him. It became more cruel. He abused his own dog. Called him 'Jesus Christ'. The man has no religion. He brags of being an atheist."

"Mr. Graham," the attorney asked, "did Elisha Kane tell you what happened at Grandview?"

"I sat down in the swing with him and asked him to tell me what happened."

"Would you tell the court what Dr. Kane told you?" Roland asked.

"He told me he was teaching Jenny how to dive in water about waist deep. She dived and came up screaming. Sash said he thought she might have struck her head against a rock. He later said he was on shore and rushed back to her, but she had gone down twice. She almost drowned him, he told me. He broke her hold and swam out."

"Is that all Dr. Kane told you, Mr. Graham?"

"By this time, I decided it wasn't necessary to ask any further questions. He couldn't get his story right."

"Did you ask that the circumstances of your daughter's death be investigated?" the Commonwealth's Attorney asked.

"No, sir. I did not know of the warrant against Dr. Kane."

Winston Read approached the witness, "Mr. Graham, why didn't you mention the cursing episodes at the coroner's investigation or the preliminary hearing?"

"I didn't think it was necessary at the time."

"Why didn't you, an associate judge of the domestic relations court of Warwick County, do something against your son-in-law when you heard him cursing and abusing your daughter?" Mr. Read asked.

"I never mentioned anything to Jenny about her life or unpleasantness with her husband. I took no action against Dr. Kane as a justice and would not have done so had I been sheriff of the county.

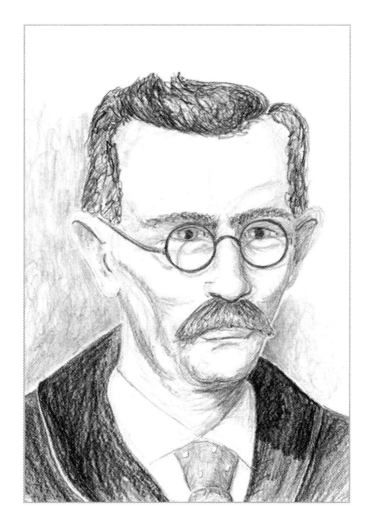

"I took no action against Dr. Kane as a justice and would not have done so had I been the sheriff of the county. Dr. Kane is large and powerful."
— *Magistrate W.C. Graham*

Dr. Kane is large and powerful. He could have carried both Jenny and myself under his arm."

"The witness is excused."

The Ambiguous Clammers

*T*he clammers were questioned. One said the screams sounded like a child's. Another said the screams sounded like a woman's, but could have been a man's. A third man said that after the screaming, which sounded like foul play, he saw someone "toting" something ashore. The person put the object on the beach, went to the automobile, backed it down and put the object in it. He said he didn't want to get mixed up in it—probably drunks. Then the man's father backed up his testimony, but when Winston Read, on cross-examination, asked about his hearing, the older man stated he was deaf. The last of the clammers to testify said the hollering sounded distressing, and he tried to see if he could hear any words, but he couldn't. The water, he said, was about pocket deep. "The man seemed in no hurry. When I saw him, he was putting on his socks or shoes."

None of the clammers could see well enough to tell who the people were—just that there were two people—not even if it was a man and a woman. They said the tide was "three-quarter ebb and dead low." None of them actually could testify to what had happened, but they thought the screaming had gone on for nearly fifteen minutes.

Sheriff Charles Curtis and his deputy, Joe Ballentine, were assigned to taking care of the jurymen. The men were comfortably quartered at the Hotel Langley on Queen Street in downtown Hampton for the duration of the trial. They were fed "the best" of food, were allowed to take a daily turn about town and go to movies as a chaperoned group. The best part of jury duty, according to a couple of men, was the opportunity to enjoy evenings at the hotel playing poker. The jurymen who served for the trial of Elisha Kane received twelve dollars and fifty cents for the five days (two-fifty a day), and they were paid in time for Christmas.

"The man seemed in no hurry. When I saw him, he was putting on his socks or shoes."

— *Fisherman*

The Mother of Fortitude

*T*he local newspaper ran a story about Golden Rule Week: "The observance is the ninth annual one, and is sponsored by the National Golden Rule Foundation." Clergy from around the nation sent out letters, asking everyone to acknowledge this special week by helping those less fortunate. "There has seldom been as much unemployment and suffering, both physical and mental, as is in prospect during the coming winter." But front-page news of the trial of the century distracted the people of the small peninsula community. Many chose not to think of the struggle that was to come. The spectacular murder case allowed them to ignore the depression.

Elisha Kane sat stone-faced in the courtroom, while other members of the Graham family took the stand to tell their stories of the miserable marriage Jenny had endured. Before Mrs. Graham's testimony, Winston Read requested the jury retire as he had a motion to present to the court. The jury filed from the room. Mr. Read stated that he understood the witness was in even worse physical condition than she was at the hearing when she collapsed. He requested that a physician examine Mrs. Graham as to her ability to testify and to stand the ordeal of a cross-examination.

Harry Smith suggested that Mrs. Graham be allowed to judge for herself if she was able to testify or not. The woman said she thought she could go through the cross-examination, and the judge agreed to let her testify only after he admonished her to maintain her composure as far as possible. Maggie Graham indicated her desire to go through the ordeal. She was helped to the witness chair.

The sixty-year-old co-founder of the chapter of the Women's Christian Temperance Union in Hilton Village, a member of both the Daughters of the Revolution and the Daughters of the Confederacy, the mother of the deceased, sat before the court. Dressed in black and having to repeatedly remove her shell-rimmed glasses to wipe away tears, she clinched her hands together around her handkerchief in an obvious effort to calm her nervous quivering. The unrestrained chattering in the courtroom ceased, and a still silence fell upon the court.

Frank, who had been so gentle with her at the hearing, stepped up to question his witness. Frank had her give her name and address for the record, and soon he began to ask her about the marital relations of her daughter and the accused.

"They were happy but Jenny feared Sash. I don't think he treated her right. Sometimes we'd hear him curse and abuse her all night. She loved him and in a way was happy, but she feared him and always was scared of him when others were around."

"How did Dr. Kane act towards you?" Frank asked.

"He was always nice to me, and I always tried to be nice to him," she answered. "I thought he might be good to Jenny if I was nice to him."

"You say the defendant had just come to town—Jenny having spent the summer months with you in Hilton Village?"

"Yes. I had dinner with Jenny and Sash at the Hotel Chamberlin on Thursday evening. We were supposed to have dinner in Hilton Village on Friday evening, but..."

Frank asked Mrs. Graham for details of the morning of September eleventh before Sash and Jenny left the house to go to

"He was always nice to me, and I tried to
be nice to him. I thought he might be good
to Jenny if I was nice to him."

— *Margaret Graham*

Grandview. She told that Sash was up early eager to leave. He went outside and worked on his car. Jenny woke later, and Mrs. Graham called Sash to come to breakfast. When he didn't answer, she went in their room. Jenny seemed to have been crying. Jenny refused to eat any breakfast—just drank half-a-glass of milk.

"Jenny didn't want to go to Grandview. I told her she didn't have to go." Mrs. Graham cried as she described her daughter's expression as she left to go to the beach as the "saddest look I'd ever seen on the face of anyone."

Frank attempted to ask the woman about confidences of Jenny to her mother, relative to relation with her husband, but the defense objected, and Judge Spratley sustained the objection.

Mrs. Graham told the court that Jenny had found quite a few letters from a woman named Dodd, or something like that, that were written to her husband. "I can recall some of the things she wrote, but I burned the letters last spring."

"What do you remember, Mrs. Graham?"

"She wanted to get rid of 'Jenny,' and she told him she would plan it and he would carry it out, and it wouldn't take much nerve to do it. She would repeatedly say she knew he loved her and not his wife. When he got rid of her, they would go away to Spain, or some country, and live together and be happy."

"Did this woman tell of a plan, Mrs. Graham?"

"I don't remember any plan, if she mentioned one at all. But they were certainly not such letters as a married man should receive." Mrs. Graham said two letters had come for Sash prior to his arrival. One was handed to him on Friday morning. Another letter, arriving in the Wednesday evening mail, Mrs. Graham handed to her daughter. "Jenny read it, or looked it over, and handed it back."

Frank then produced the infamous "Betty" letter.

Winston Read was on his feet in an instant. "I object to the admission of this letter…"

Judge Spratley called order to the room of spectators tete-a-teting with each other. "The jury will be excused, while the court considers the objection."

Once the twelve jurors were out of the courtroom, the judge asked Frank, "Was the letter addressed to the accused by a third person?"

"Yes, Your Honor."

"Then the letter is not evidence," Judge Spratley said. "According to testimony of your witness, Mr. Kearney, that letter was not seen or delivered to the accused."

Newsmen scurried to get the news out. "Judge Rules Out Letters Held As State's Bulwark." A disappointed sigh grew from amongst the spectators as word passed about the room. "He is not allowing the letters to be presented in court." Judge Spratley called for order and asked that the jury be called back.

Mr. Read approached the witness, "Mrs. Graham, you said you had dinner with your daughter and her husband Thursday evening?"

"Yes, at the Hotel Chamberlin."

"Was this pleasant?"

"Yes, sir," she answered.

"Mrs. Graham, is it unusual for Jenny to go without breakfast?"

"Often Jenny ate lightly."

"Mrs. Graham," Mr. Read continued, "did Jenny eat breakfast on the day previous to the tragedy?"

The woman spoke softly, "I'm not sure."

"Was Dr. Kane nice to you only sometimes, or was he uniformly nice to you, Mrs. Graham?"

"Dr. Kane was uniformly nice to me."

"That is all," Mr. Read said.

"You are excused, Mrs. Graham. Thank you," Judge Spratley said.

The woman readjusted her glasses once more, and the bailiff held her arm and walked her to the jury box door. She had held herself well on the stand. A reporter noted she had answered questions "carefully and deliberately."

The Persevering Accuser

"*T*he State calls Mr. W. H. Graham to the stand." The judge swiveled his chair so that he was facing the wall behind the bench. Perhaps he felt he could better determine the truth without the expressions of the witnesses. Or did he not want his expressions to give away his own leanings? With few exceptions, the judge only faced the court when he needed to address the court, but there was no doubt he heard every word spoken.

"You are the brother of the deceased, Mr. Graham?" Mr. Smith asked.

"Yes, sir. Jenny was my sister." Hop Graham was a youthful looking man with a pointy nose and a receding chin. He said he was a fish house manager for L.M. Newcomb.

"How long have you known the defendant?"

"About thirteen years," Hop Graham answered, avoiding the grim stare of the professor.

"Mr. Graham, you are familiar with the defendant's automobile?"

"Yes, sir."

"Can you tell us if the license plate has the name "Tennessee" in full or if it is abbreviated?"

"I don't know."

"Do you know if Virginia is spelled out on the license plates?" Mr. Smith asked.

"No, sir. I don't know."

"That's all right, Mr. Graham." The lawyer dropped the subject without making clear what he had been trying to do with it.

"Let me ask about something else. How would you describe the relationship of the defendant and your sister?"

"In the past six years I've noticed a marked change in Jenny. She was fearful and particularly ill at ease in the presence of her husband. He tried to keep her away from us," Hop said.

"Go on."

"She loved him dearly. No one ever loved a person more than she loved him. She tried to shield his treatment of her."

"Mr. Graham, how do you know your sister was afraid of her husband?" Mr. Smith asked.

"When anything happened… like she had an accident with the car. Jenny hurried to have it repaired before Sash found out about it."

"The defense has no questions for this witness," Percy said.

One of the jurymen asked if he might ask the witness a question.

"Go ahead," the judge said.

"Was your sister as tall as you, Mr. Graham? And what was her weight?"

"I believe she was about as tall as I am, and I guess she weighed about a hundred-and-forty-five pounds."

Jenny's sister, Mrs. Pauline Webber, was the next witness. She testified that Jenny had never liked to get her head wet and seldom went into the water. "She preferred to take a sun bath on the beach." Mrs. Webber said she had visited Jenny in Chapel Hill and that the relations between Jenny and Sash were not pleasant.

The prosecution announced that Mr. Wilbur Hudgins would be their last witness. Mr. Hudgins' wife had testified on the preceding day. He told of the day Jenny had come crying to them because Sash had told her he was interested in another woman and had even shown her a photo of the woman. This was in the summer of

"What would be sufficient bail for an ordinary prisoner would not be sufficient bail for the scion of a prominent and wealthy Pennsylvania family."

— *Roland Cock*

1929. "Jenny came to us saying Sash didn't want her to go back to Knoxville with him."

"The prosecution rests."

The jury was asked to leave the courtroom while Winston Read presented a motion.

"Your Honor, I respectfully make the motion the court dismiss the case on the grounds the melodramatic evidence produced by the Commonwealth is not sufficient to sustain a verdict of guilty. The evidence is conflicting and unreliable, and not a single witness has testified the defendant held the victim under water until she drowned. The proof is not sufficient to justify a verdict against the accused."

Roland Cock pushed his chair back. He slowly unfolded his rumpled self. He approached the bench. "Your Honor, the victim came to her death while in the company of her husband, the defendant. Eyewitnesses heard cries of distress and the presence of one or more of the principals in the water. The defendant told several conflicting stories. The tides and currents were contradictory to his stories regarding his efforts to save his wife."

Judge Spratley refused to dismiss the case. The defense team would have to call their witnesses.

The Professor's Advocates

*A*mong the witnesses for the defense was a number of former Commonwealth witnesses who were not certain what they saw was a deliberate drowning of a woman by a man. Friends of the professor were there to sharply contradict the testimony of the State's witnesses. The defense had a parade of character witnesses lined up to tell of the happy relations between the Kanes.

The first witness for the defense was Dr. Harry D. Howe of Dixie Hospital who testified about the professor bringing his wife to the hospital. He told that Sash had insisted they try to resuscitate his wife; he tried but was unable to do so. He said in applying the usual efforts at resuscitation, a quantity of water came from the lungs. He believed she had died from drowning.

Dr. Howe was asked, "Is it possible for the victim to have died from heart trouble, and if so, would there have been any water in the lungs."

"Yes, water would enter the lungs in such an event, but it is impossible to say how much water would enter.

"I cannot say if I got all the water out of her lungs," the doctor added.

Next the wife of a University of North Carolina professor testified. "Dr. Kane took a room in my home in September of 1927," Mrs. John T. Lear said. "When Jenny, Mrs. Kane, came, the couple took a house about two hundred yards away. They always appeared to be very happy. An ideal married couple."

"Mrs. Lear, did you have any reason to think Jenny Kane had health problems?"

"On Easter morning, about 8:30, Jenny called me. She said she was dying. I rushed to the Kanes' home and found Jenny slumped in a chair holding her hand over her heart. She said she was dying, but she wouldn't let me call a doctor. She insisted her husband's father was treating her."

"Did you think …"

"Objection," Frank called out. "What this witness thinks…"

"I withdraw my question," Mr. Read said. "Thank you, Mrs. Lear. No further questions."

The State had no questions for Mrs. Lear. She was dismissed.

"The Kanes' sleeping porch was within hearing of my bedroom," Mr. Adams, also from Chapel Hill, North Carolina, testified. "Had there been any swearing, I could have heard it. I never heard any cursing or offensive language. Dr. Kane was always very considerate of his wife."

The defense called Dr. Dewey Peters of Knoxville.

"Dr. Peters, did you know Mrs. Jenny Kane?"

"I saw Mrs. Kane in April of this year. It was for a consultation. She filled out a report for me. On it she said she was suffering from a point in the back region of the kidneys, that she took soda often, that she had been suffering from an inward goiter and that she was easily exhausted and ran a temperature."

"And what was your diagnosis, Dr. Peters?" Mr. Read asked.

"I did not completely diagnose the case. Mrs. Kane did not return to my office as I expected. I recall her telling me she was ambitious and energetic and prided herself on doing things efficiently and snappy, but, she said, after doing them, she would be depressed."

Another witness, Mr. Willis D. Holloway, a clammer, said, "I heard hollering, which seemed to be a man's voice. I saw a man take a body to the beach, back up an automobile and drive off rapidly."

When Mr. Holloway's son was on the stand, the seventeen-year-old boy was cross-examined by the State. A reporter explained later,

"The boy was harried and beset by questions of counsel framed in words which doubtless the boy had never heard. He swore he had never talked over the case with anyone nor told anyone what he had seen, not even his 'pop.' It was easily apparent he would not have been there if this were true... it seemed a pity he should be made the target for such an attack from the State counsel."

Mrs. Esther Kimball of Buckroe Beach said the Kane car passed her at terrific speed. "So fast that it had to pass a streetcar on the left."

Mr. L.L. Bradford of Hampton said he was driving between forty and forty-five miles an hour when the Kane car passed him between Hampton and Phoebus. "The almost continuous horn was what attracted me."

Mr. W.J. Smith of the funeral parlor where Mrs. Kane's body was taken said Mr. Kane looked at his wife, threw his hands to his face and collapsed.

Mr. Lee Ryan of Knoxville said he frequently visited the Kanes and thought they were congenial and happy. Mrs. C. S. Price and Mrs. Lee Ragsdale said the relations of the Kanes were harmonious. Professor and Mrs. Stratton Buck and Professor Walter Stevens of the University vouched for the Kane's good relationship. Mr. Lee Ragsdale and Mr. T. C. Walker also spoke of the good relationship of the husband and wife. When asked, these witnesses said they had seen nothing to indicate Jenny Kane feared her husband.

The defense called Dr. E. A. Abernathy, who was in charge of the infirmary at the University of North Carolina. "I treated Mrs. Kane many times for various illnesses during a two-year period." He said she had suffered six or eight heart attacks—several of them very definite heart attacks.

"During these attacks," the doctor told the jury, "Mrs. Kane complained of pains, her breathing was difficult, and she had a very fast pulse, irregular at times. Her heart action was tumultuous at times, and she suffered from weakening of the muscles of the heart. I found Mrs. Kane to be an unfortunate woman who had a gloomy outlook on life, especially when suffering from heart trouble."

When questioned, Dr. Abernathy said, "If she had suffered one of her attacks while on the rocks at Grandview Beach, Mrs. Kane would have been unable to take care of herself."

Harry Smith cross-examined the witness. "Doctor, would you believe Mrs. Kane had been cured of heart trouble if reputable physicians had examined her and pronounced her cured three weeks before her death?"

"I doubt that people ever get over heart disease," Dr. Abernathy replied.

Roy Phillips, a juryman, asked the doctor if people suffering in this manner could have strength enough to fight off someone trying to help them.

"Persons in such a condition are unable to collect themselves. They are panicky and show unusual strength."

Another juryman, Louis MacVicar, asked the doctor if unhappy living conditions could have affected her heart. Dr. Abernathy replied such would not have any effect on the heart, "but her nervous condition would."

Mrs. Susan Lee of Hilton Village was the next witness called by the defense.

"Mrs. Lee, was the deceased in your shop in September of this year?" Mr. Read asked.

"Yes, sir. She came in during the early part of the week of her death." The witness sat on the edge of the chair and all but shouted her response.

"Please, go on, Mrs. Lee."

"Well, Mrs. Kane said she wanted to see an old picture that I had on the second floor. She started up the stairs—mind you,

"Some people will always believe him guilty."

— *Newsman*

they are very steep—and I was behind her. Well, she fell back into my arms."

"She fell, you say?"

"Yes, sir. Mrs. Kane had a heart attack and she fell…"

"Objection. The witness is drawing a conclusion," the prosecutor said.

Mrs. Lee slid back in the witness chair and lowered her head.

"Please, just tell us what happened, Mrs. Lee," Mr. Read smiled kindly at the witness.

"Well," Mrs. Lee spoke more timidly, "Mrs. Kane was entirely unconscious. For five, or six minutes. It took me some time to get her to a chair. I got some ammonia and water. She took some kind of pill she had in her bag."

"Thank you, Mrs. Lee."

Dr. E. W. Camm of Durham, North Carolina, presented X-ray photographs of Mrs. Kane's heart. He and Dr. W. R. Staunton, also of Durham, supported Dr. Abernathy's testimony. "Her heart had a rapid beat with a rate of 108."

Two fishermen who had seen Sash at Grandview and an insurance man and a druggist from Hilton Village testified for the defense. A surveyor, Mr. W.T. Darden, had gone to the scene of the drowning. He testified that he had slipped on the rocks while there. He said there were several holes near the rocks where the water was deeper after a change from ebb tide.

The Esteemed Doctor

*T*he prosecution had given the Graham family members an opportunity to express themselves on the witness stand. At last it was Dr. Evan Kane's turn to speak. One of the nation's most noted surgeons walked swiftly to the front of the courtroom with the eagerness of a politician towards the grand stand in the city park.

"Dr. Kane," Percy addressed him, "when did you first meet your son's wife, Jenny Graham Kane?"

"It was shortly after their marriage. Sash and Jenny were still honeymooning when they came to see me in Pennsylvania."

"The couple did not make their home in Pennsylvania. Did you have an opportunity to get to know Jenny Kane?"

"Most certainly," Dr. Kane answered. "They would visit occasionally. When visiting with me, they would occupy the room directly across the hall from me."

"Were you ever aware of loud voices coming come their room?" Percy asked.

"The two of them were extremely cordial to each other, Mr. Carmel. I never heard them arguing, and I certainly never heard any cursing." The little man looked about the courtroom as if he wanted to be sure everyone heard what he had said. Percy waited until Dr. Kane, indicating he was satisfied, gave a turn of his head.

"What can you tell us about your daughter-in-law?" Percy asked.

"Jenny was very nervous. She suffered from functional heart disease," Dr. Kane answered.

"'Functional heart disease,'" Percy repeated his words. "Can you explain?"

"Yes, her heart gradually enlarged, and she developed a leakage in the right side, which caused what is referred to as a functional nervous heart."

"Were you her physician, Dr. Kane?"

"My son and his wife didn't live in Kane, but when they would visit, she would call me at night saying her heart had stopped beating."

"And what would you do?"

"At first I would come running at any time of the night. I would assure them that everything was alright and tell them I needed my sleep." There was a stir in the courtroom, and Judge Spratley tapped his gavel.

"You mean you didn't find anything wrong with Jenny?" Percy asked.

"Her heart would be floundering and flopping, but she needed to calm down."

"And did she, calm down?" Percy asked.

"As time went on, she became worse. Her heart did not pump evenly and smoothly."

Dr. Kane explained, "This uneven contracting did not expulse the blood correctly."

"Dr. Kane, how long have you practiced medicine?" Percy asked.

"I have been a physician directly since 1884 and indirectly since ten years before."

"Did you serve in the Great War?"

"I was too old to get overseas. They kept me in a training camp. I guess I made a fool of myself among all those youngsters," the doctor said whimsically.

"And you have…"

"If it pleases the court," Frank Kearney interrupted, "the State and everyone here recognizes the highly esteemed doctor."

"Thank you, Mr. Kearney," Judge Spratley said.

"Did you recommend some treatment for Jenny?" Percy asked Dr. Kane.

"It was my opinion if a person continually—for a long period of time—believed he or she had heart trouble, it was possible for this ailment to develop. There is a case on record of this kind."

"Then, you are saying, Jenny was so alarmed over her irregular heartbeat, she in fact made her condition worse?" Percy asked the elderly doctor.

"Mr. Carmel, my son used to lie with his head on her breast. He did not get any sleep. I did not get any sleep. I censured him for babying her."

There was some discussion of the late hour when the defense finished with Dr. Kane, and so the court was adjourned. As Dr. Kane left the stand, he turned to Judge Spratley and asked him to excuse him for taking so much time in testifying. He said, "I'm very interested in that little boy," and he looked at Sash.

The "little boy" towered over his father as a Bullmastiff towers over a Chihuahua. Dr. Kane had won the favor of the courtroom full of people. They were impressed that he was a world-renowned doctor, and they saw him as an enchanting, elfish man stepping up to speak on behalf of his son. It was easy to judge Sash and Tom and, even Kent Kane, as young, whippersnappers from the North, but not this dear little man.

On the next day when the burly Mr. Smith stood to cross-examine Dr. Kane, he looked rather like a lion about to devour a defenseless creature. The courtroom fell silent. Mr. Smith acknowledged the witness, "Dr. Kane, I appreciate your presence in the court today."

Dr. Kane nodded.

"Your son, Dr. Elisha Kent Kane, sits before this court accused of the drowning death of his young wife," Mr. Smith continued.

"I know how difficult it must be for you to come here today..."

"It would be impossible for me not to come..." Dr Kane offered.

"Of course, as his father, you must be most upset by all this. But let's be honest, Dr. Kane—you and your son have not been on the best of terms."

"My son is a highly respected college professor," Dr. Kane enunciated these words.

"Yes, sir," said Mr. Smith, "but didn't this college professor send you a harsh letter recently?"

"I do not know what you refer to," Dr. Kane replied.

"I refer to this letter I hold in my hand."

"Objection!" Percy Carmel stood. Judge Spratley had the jury removed while the admission of a letter was argued between the counselors.

"Such a letter would be immaterial," the judge declared. "Objection sustained. The jury may return."

Mr. Smith attempted to question Dr. Kane about the health of his daughter-in-law. "Did Mrs. Kane have any heart lesions?"

"I did detect a blowing murmur at my last examination," Dr. Kane said. "I believe some specialist," he said with distain, "had used an electrical apparatus in treating her heart trouble. I believe this treatment is not of benefit to the patient, but can be dangerous."

Mr. Smith returned to the prosecutor's table to pick up a medical book. "I wish to read from this medical text published just last year..."

"I would caution you not to think you can understand such a text without a great deal of study, Mr. Smith. Have you a medical degree?"

There was a chuckle in the courtroom, but Mr. Smith continued to read.

"You haven't pronounced that right, sir," Dr. Kane interrupted. "Don't pick out paragraphs. You must read the whole text to enlighten yourself, and the court. It is not fair to try to use brief extracts."

Mr. Smith closed the medical book and, casually placing it back on the table, tried another approach.

"Dr. Kane, what did you think of your daughter-in-law?"

"Jenny was a very talented woman…"

"Dr. Kane, you did not think Mrs. Kane had heart troubles, isn't that correct?"

"For the first five or six years, I did not realize the root of Mrs. Kane's trouble."

"Which was?" the counselor prompted the witness.

"She had a fundamental heart disorder," the doctor answered. "During these attacks her pulse became rapid and her heart very weak. I could hardly hear her heart through the stethoscope.

"My son was concerned over his wife's condition. Consequently his work suffered. Mrs. Kane had an overwhelming fear of death. During these attacks she would cry, 'Oh, Sash, save me. I'm dying.'

"I remember one day I was walking with them in the woods. Mrs. Kane was taken with an attack," the attorney allowed Dr. Kane to continue. "She fell to the ground. My son dropped to his knees beside her and cried, 'Oh, Baby, Baby, don't die.' We carried Mrs. Kane back to the house, and my son refused to leave her. He administered to her wants for three days. And," the old man concluded, "that was only one of many examples of constant care and devotion my son showed his wife."

"Dr. Kane," Mr. Smith was growing impatient with the witness, "did Mrs. Kane have a toxic goiter?"

"Several physicians thought so, but I do not know."

"Have you talked with Dr. E.A. Abernethy, Dr. Kane? You remember, the doctor who testified Mrs. Kane suffered from heart attacks…" Mr. Smith added.

"Of course, I did," Dr. Kane answered. "So why ask me? Tell me, Mr. Smith, have you ever been diagnosed with cholangitis?"

"No, I haven't," Mr. Smith replied peevishly.

"You may, Mr. Smith," the doctor said, "as you are getting old."

The two old men bandied words for half-an-hour. Then Smith apparently surmised that anything more from this witness would not benefit the State. He turned to the judge, "I have no further questions for this witness."

"Dr. Kane," Judge Spratley said, "you are excused."

"Please," the doctor addressed the judge, "may I be permitted to show the jury something?"

It was a copy of the New Testament given to him by his son, Professor Kane. "My son gave this to me and requested that I always keep it with me. The prosecution has presented testimony that would make it appear my son has no religion and actually boasts of not being so superstitious as to have any fear of God."

The judge allowed the defendant's father to show the New Testament to the jury. "Contrary to what has been said in this court," the elderly man addressed the jury, "Professor Kane is a member of the Presbyterian Church."

The Brother of Kane

*T*he defense called Dr. Thomas L. Kane. Mr. Read asked the fundamental questions so the information would be entered in the record. Thomas was a brother of the defendant. He had known Jenny Kane for thirteen years. He had received a medical education from the University of Chicago and had spent ten months in the special study of the heart.

"How would you describe your sister-in-law, Dr. Kane?"

"Jenny was a charming woman," Thomas said. "She was a fine conversationalist. I was very fond of her."

"Did you have an opportunity to consider Mrs. Kane's health?"

"My sister-in-law suffered from attacks. She was taking large amounts of patent medicines and digitalis."

"Were you ever present when Mrs. Kane had an attack, Dr. Kane?"

"I have seen Jenny in hysteria at least a hundred times."

"A hundred?"

Dr. Kane nodded. "Sometimes the attack would run three minutes. Sometimes, as long as ten minutes."

"And what did you attribute these attacks to?" Mr. Read asked.

"I finally concluded that Jenny's hysteria was due to a heart condition." Dr. Kane backed up this statement with great detail, and with no interruptions from the State.

"You told us, Dr. Kane, that you took special courses of study at the University of Chicago?" Mr. Read asked.

"Yes, as I said, ten months concentrating on studies of the heart."

"Dr. Kane, how would you say Dr. and Mrs. Kane got along?"

"My brother and his wife had many things in common, both being poetic and artistic. They did not draw apart as the years went on. She would paint and write, while he was studying. They had a great variety of pet names for each other. I rather thought they overdid it. They lived and loved for each other."

"Thank you, Dr. Kane. That is all."

The prosecution had no questions for Thomas.

"Gentlemen," Judge Spratley addressed the counselors at both tables, "the court has several other cases on the docket for Monday. This case must be completed this week. If necessary, I will have to call a night session."

The Defendant Takes the Stand

*P*erhaps sales of candy canes and toy trucks were down the Christmas of 1931 due to the Depression, but newspaper sales were up in the Hampton area. Newsboys had little trouble selling their bundles of papers during the week of the murder trial. Mr. Fertitta did a volume of business selling lunches to the attendees, and Langley Hotel on Queen Street was booked by the "Fourth Estate," the people of the press. H.G. Proctor represented the *Philadelphia Bulletin,* and Leighton H. Blood was in town for the *Washington Herald.* Dorothy Ducas, a twenty-six year old from New York, was covering the story for the International News Service. Though young, Dorothy had a resume that included the *New York Herald Tribune* and the *Evening Post.*

The stories Dorothy wrote were published in the *Kane Republican* in the small Pennsylvania town where Sash was born. Dorothy had a byline on her stories. She wrote candidly of what she witnessed at the trial of Sash Kane. Dorothy said the hostility of Jenny's family towards the professor "excited the comment of friends… even intimates of the Grahams are mystified at the complete right-about-face in the attitude of the woman's family." She said people had thought the family was on the best of terms with the son-in-law right up to the time of the drowning. Jenny's aunt had protested; "But he couldn't have done it. He was devoted to her."

On December 11, Dorothy wrote of Sash's testimony at the trial:
Every spectator in the court room leaned forward expectantly as he began the story of his life in a deep, cultured voice.

Sash told of his childhood, his education, his marriage and his career.

It was an unusually warm day for December—as warm as a late May day. The courtroom was crowded, and beads of moisture dotted the foreheads of everyone in the court. Still Sash kept his double-breasted coat buttoned. He sat upright in the hard court chair. Looking imperturbable, he faced the men of the jury in whose hands his fate lay.

Sash told the court he had taught summer school at the University of Tennessee and then went to Camp Bragg before coming to Virginia. I hurried to get here "a day early to surprise Jenny."

Sash said Jenny had written to him saying she had learned to swim. She was anxious to show him. They went to Virginia Beach. "Jenny could float," the husband testified, "although she was nervous, and she could do a sort of scissors stroke which was not very good."

He said she was still bothered at getting her head wet. He tried to help her telling her to hold her nose and put her head in the water while he held her hand. "She did this, but she didn't like it. I held her hand all the time," Dorothy quoted the professor.

Sash explained that Jenny was embarrassed when other people were around. They had always liked to go down by the lighthouse when they went to Grandview. They would sit in the shade of the lighthouse to eat their lunch.

According to Sash, Jenny had had a headache the morning of her death. Neither of them had slept well the night before as it was extremely hot. They had stopped at a drug store on the way to the beach to get something for her headache. He said Jenny hadn't wanted to eat that morning because what her mother had prepared was greasy.

The Back River Lighthouse at Grandview

Dorothy quoted Sash's version of what had happened at the beach for the news service:

"She fell in... I swam as fast as I could...she held on convulsively... I got an arm hold on her... it seemed as if the whole weight of the ocean was pressing against me... I screamed for help until I was hoarse... none of the boatmen responded... Jenny went limp, as if she fainted.

"I laid my wife on the beach," Elisha Kane continued. The jurors listened intently as he spoke. They watched him with round, solemn eyes, leaning forward in their chairs—they were a perfect audience.

Dorothy continued to quote Sash:
"I backed the car, and put her in the seat. This was the hardest part. I called to her 'Baby, Baby,

Baby, pick up your feet.' I loved the woman I couldn't save... I kept my foot on the accelerator right down to the floor all the way—at no time did I loiter. I drove like the devil.

"It seemed nobody at the hospital knew what to do." Sash wept.
"I thought she was dying. I didn't realize she was dead."

Mr. Smith began with a brisk and sharp cross-examination of the accused professor. He asked Sash if he had heard the testimony given by the sheriff, members of the Graham family and others.
Sash said he had.

"Then you are calling them liars by denying the truthfulness of their statements? The clammers. Were they also lying?"

"They might have been mistaken. The fact they testified what they thought they saw and heard does not imply any intention on my part to call them liars."

Mr. Read objected to the nature of Mr. Smith's questioning, and Judge Spratley warned Mr. Smith that such questions were dangerously near the illegal limits.

At one time during his cross-examination, Sash bolted from the witness chair, waving his hands and vehemently denying he had used profanity with his wife.

"I may have cursed other people and other things," he said. "I may have let out a healthy damn once in a while, but curse her! Never in my life! I couldn't. She was too dear to me. That is a damnable lie that was cooked up against me."

Sash went pale and grim-lipped. He returned to the witness chair and apologized for his outburst, "Pardon me, Judge, but my life for three months has been hell."

Mr. Smith turned the questioning to the woman Sash had admitted having with him at the Army base.

"Yes, I did invite Mrs. Betty Dahl to attend dances with me at the camp and after that I was with her in Atlantic City."

"What rank do you hold at the present time?" Mr. Smith asked of his military career.

"I am a major in the Organized Reserves."

"Dr. Kane," the lawyer for the State asked, "haven't you a pretty violent temper?"

"No, I do not."

"Are you always cool and collected?" the attorney pressed.

"No," Sash replied.

Percy asked Dr. Paul J. Parker of Hampton if he would say a person had died from drowning if he had seen such a person in a hospital and only a quart of water was taken from the body.

The doctor answered, "No human being on earth could tell whether Mrs. Kane died of drowning, or heart trouble without a properly performed autopsy."

Roland Cock then asked Dr. Parker, "Would you state whether a person had been drowned if the person had been overboard, was going down for the third time, had been seized around the neck and head, had been carried ashore, efforts made to get water from the body and then been taken to a hospital?"

Mr. Read stood and added to Mr. Cock's list of conditions, "And the person was subject to hysteria, had been seen to fall from a rock and screamed."

"No one could tell the cause of death under such circumstances," the doctor repeated.

The defense closed their case with the hour-long testimony of Dr. J. Wilton Hope who described the differences between hysteria and heart disease.

The Encore for the Prosecution

The prosecutor had the Grahams return to deny any knowledge of Jenny having heart trouble. Her sister said Jenny had sinus trouble and that she had never seen her have a heart attack, nor had she ever seen her unconscious. Mrs. Graham said she never heard her daughter complain of heart trouble. While on the stand, Mrs. Graham claimed she had heard Sash Kane cursing repeatedly. "And," she said, "none of my children ever complained of meals served them, or of poorly cooked or greasy food."

Mr. Graham reiterated no knowledge of Jenny complaining of her heart, but on cross-examination, when asked if he knew certain physicians, he said he did not remember any "heart attacks except once Dr. J. Kennedy Corss visited my daughter."

Dr. Corss, a Newport News physician and surgeon, was called to testify. He said he had attended Mrs. Kane numerous times and that, while she imagined she had heart trouble, he never had discovered any evidence. He said "she was a pitiful neurasthenic with an obsession for sickness."

Hop Graham paused in his testimony to glare at the man he accused of killing Jenny. Sash had said Hop had struck him when he was handcuffed. Hop denied this. He said he had not instituted the prosecution, but he was paying part of the cost for employing the eminent lawyers who were assisting the Commonwealth.

Coroner Vanderslice was called by the State to answer whether Dr. Evan Kane had testified at the hearing that he had prescribed digitalis for Mrs. Kane. He said Dr. Kane had so testified and had said his son's wife had no organic heart trouble, but that she had functional heart disease. The stern Dixie Hospital doctor, who had failed to do an autopsy, was spared another cross-examination and was dismissed.

The State and the defense had more testimony presented regarding the depth of the water at the time of the drowning. Each had expert witnesses to prove his point.

The Defense rested. Something like one hundred witnesses had been summoned by the State and the defense. Only about half of them had been called to appear. Telegraph boys darted in and out a rear door to send the word to news offices: The lawyers would be giving the summations when court reconvened.

Meanwhile, Hop was shouting from an upper window of the courthouse. The Graham ladies were having a confrontation with press photographers on the rear steps of the courthouse. "If they keep it up, break the camera!" Hop coaxed his wife.

Metta Graham battled with the photographers who were insisting on flashing a picture of the senior Mrs. Graham. She kicked one camera, knocked another to the ground, pulled the coat from one man and swung wildly at another while Hop urged her on and promised to join in the fray. A camera was smashed and a photographer received a scratch on his nose.

The newspapers reported the story though, of course, they had no photos of the incident. Metta was quoted:
"I did it to shield my mother-in-law from further annoyance as she had become hysterical when she was photographed previously, and the flashlight exploded."

Dorothy Ducas did not witness the plight of her colleagues. She was busy lining up an interview with Sash.

The Adversaries' Last Stand

*T*he "private prosecutor," as he called himself, was the first counsel to give his closing remarks to the jury. Mr. Smith explained that someone was lying. Either the accused was lying, or the Grahams and the fishermen were lying. "I think you can judge the temperament and the temper of the accused by the exhibition he gave on the witness stand."

The attorney for the State said, "When the screams sounded, only one person would appear in the water. Then there would be two more screams and one figure… Gentlemen, I cannot believe you men will say that Elisha Kane, III, is the only person who has told the truth here on the stand—that these God-fearing men, these fisherman, would lie."

Mr. Smith said, "In the face of all the direct evidence given by witnesses from Hilton Village, there was no necessity to show motive." He said evidence showed the defendant had cursed and abused his wife, and he admitted being with another woman in Fort Bragg and Atlantic City. When the jury summed up all the testimony, Mr. Smith said, they would render a verdict of conviction.

Percy was the first to speak for the defense.

"Do you," he asked the jury, "believe Professor Kane came to Hilton Village with any murderous motives? Do you believe his relations with his wife were not pleasing and loving? All the evidence to suggest such comes from the Graham family. The testimony of neighbors and friends in Knoxville and Chapel Hill, covering a period of five years, indicates the relations between Dr. Kane and his wife were those of extreme fondness and love for each other.

"Please," he handed the jurors letters, "read carefully the letters from Mrs. Kane to her husband. Note the enduring names used, such as 'Darling Boy Blue,' 'Precious,' 'My own love bird,' and many others. Do these words sound like the words of a woman who is in deathly fear of her husband … as the Graham family testified?"

Percy asked the jurors to consider the testimony of those who saw Professor Kane speeding towards the hospital, the statements of doctors who treated Jenny, and the x-ray that showed an enlargement of the heart.

"The Commonwealth," Percy said, "has sought to prove Mrs. Kane was held under the water. How was that possible without a mark being found on her body? The Commonwealth holds that she was drowned, yet you have heard physicians testify that nobody in this world could tell if she drowned, or if she died of heart disease without an autopsy. They did not make an autopsy. The Commonwealth has not proven its case. They have not successfully combated the evidence of the defendant and his witnesses. They have not acted as though they themselves thought they could prove that Mrs. Kane was murdered. I ask that a verdict of acquittal be rendered."

Frank approached the jury for the State. He asked them how a man who loved his wife so dearly did not hesitate to allow her to spend practically half of her time at the Graham home. "She was away from him, according to the evidence, six months in 1930 and from June 1, up to the time of her death in 1931."

"This man is a 'Dr. Jekyll and Mr. Hyde,'" Frank said. "He treated his wife with every consideration while in the company of others, except her family, and at other times abused her like a dog."

The prosecutor said Professor Kane seemed to have convenient memory loses. His statements regarding his wife's drowning were inconsistent. He changed his statement from several hundred yards to sixty, or seventy.

Frank disclaimed that any malice had been shown by the Graham family and added that Hop Graham was not responsible for the prosecution. "The prosecution was based on information that reached the Commonwealth's attorney by the clammers who had heard screams and witnessed the struggle in the waters of Chesapeake Bay on the morning of September 11."

He closed by telling the jurors they didn't have to decide whether Mrs. Kane died from drowning or heart trouble, but whether she died at the hands of the professor. "The matter before you is quite serious. I hope you will give the accused the same consideration you would give any other man. If you believe the witnesses of the Commonwealth, bring in a verdict commensurate with the old maxim, 'Whosoever sheddeth man's blood, by man shall his blood be shed.'"

Mr. Winston Read gave the next address. "The issue set forth by the court to you, the jury, was that you must believe beyond a shadow of the doubt that the accused feloniously, willfully, and with malicious aforethought, held his wife under the waters of the Chesapeake Bay until she drowned.

"Who says that the prisoner held his wife under the waters of the Chesapeake Bay?" Mr. Read said with spirit and emphasis. "Not one of the witnesses said so."

"The visibility was clear. It was a perfect day and, if the spot was lonesome, it was not lonesome that day. The Commonwealth wants you to believe the accused took his wife down to a spot in plain view of the boatmen, in daytime, and drowned her. This is absurd."

Mr. Read pointed out to the jury that the watermen who were closest to the people had testified the screams were those of a man. "It would be a shame and a reproach on my adopted land if you bring back a conviction on the evidence presented."

The one who had brought the accused to trial, Roland Cock, was the last of the attorneys to speak. He questioned the statement of the accused regarding his keeping his wife's head above water while pulling her to the beach. He referred to the Kane family as dramatic and forceful. He thought Dr. Kane's display of the New Testament and his calling the defendant "that little boy" theatrical.

He said, "The clammers saw two people in water that was never more than pocket deep. Whose word is there to take?" Mr. Cock asked the jury. "That of Professor Kane, who has something at stake, or that of the clammers, who are disinterested?"

Mr. Cock said, "Evidence showed Professor Kane drove fast in thickly settled places and slowly in others. Later he said she must have hit her head on a rock, having no idea then of attributing the death to a heart attack. He had to wait until after she was drowned before saying anything about a heart attack."

"When the clammers came to me," Mr. Cock continued, "I had to order the sheriff to arrest Professor Kane, or give up my job. The professor referred to the alleged heart trouble as an afterthought, pure and simple.

"Elisha Kent Kane has repeatedly contradicted his statements and can't be believed," the prosecutor said. "Out of his own mouth Elisha Kane has been convicted as a falsifier. We have proven this woman came to her death at the hands of Elisha Kent Kane, and I want you to punish him for what he is, a wife murderer."

The Optimistic Journalist

*D*orothy Ducas wrote:

> He is a strange man, this raw-boned sunburned professor whom I
> had occasion to observe for ten days, steadily. Undeniably charming,
> he is also rather puzzling. A man not easily open to interpretation.

Judge Spratley had charged the jurors. "In view of the peculiar-
ities of the State's case, only two verdicts are possible: guilty of
murder in the first degree, or acquittal." He told the men that
circumstantial evidence is legal and competent and entitled to the
same weight as direct testimony. He said it wasn't necessary to
show intent to kill prior to the time of the killing.

"If you bring in a verdict of guilty," he told them, "you must
believe the accused with his hands did willfully and feloniously
immerse his wife in the waters of the Chesapeake Bay. If you
believe she slipped, or fell, or dived into the water and was thereby
drowned, you will find him not guilty."

What followed was a buzzing about that would outdo the
busiest beehive. Dorothy and her colleagues had listened intently
to the summations and studied the twelve faces of the jury. Now
they hastened to predict an acquittal.

Dorothy wrote:

Professor Elisha Kent Kane, III, will be a free man tonight or completely bowled over by an absolutely unexpected verdict. He has not the faintest notion of conviction. He never had. The husky University of Tennessee professor confidently waits for vindication.

Not only has he told a logical, a plausible, version of his actions on the beach that day when his wife tumbled off the rocks at Back River lighthouse, but the Commonwealth has failed to bring out any motive for possible murder. That they hoped to do, of course, with the introduction of the 'Betty' letters—the epistles Professor Kane's alleged sweetheart wrote him.

Dorothy reminded the readers:

The court ruled them out as evidence three times, for the prosecuting lawyers doggedly kept bringing them back.

Dorothy said the defense had built its case on the character witnesses who knew the Kanes had a happy relationship, a series of medical experts declaring the woman suffered from a heart malady, and eyewitnesses from Back River to Dixie Hospital.

It should not take the jury long to bring in its verdict.

As it was five-thirty when Judge Spratley charged the jury, he told them they might go to dinner before starting their deliberations. They returned at eight o'clock. Deputy Clerk Giddings turned over to the foreman all the instructions, the letters and other papers. It was then that the jury retired.

The judge called the jurors back to the courtroom at eleven o'clock. "Have you reached a verdict?"

"No, we have not," the foreman answered.

"Unless you have reached a verdict by twelve o'clock, I will have to adjourn you over to Monday, as I cannot receive a verdict on Sunday. I know you are weary, but there is nothing else I can do."

"All I can say now, Judge," Foreman Louis MacVicar replied, "is that we have not agreed upon a verdict. Will you give us until eleven-thirty?"

The judge acquiesced. The jurors again retired.

At eleven-forty-five there was a knock on the door of the jury room. The courtroom spectators responded as they would to the rapping of the judge's gavel. The door was opened, and the jury filed in. One or two of them was smiling.

"Have you agreed on a verdict, gentlemen?" the judge asked.

"We have," the foreman replied.

"What is it?" Judge Spratley asked.

"We had expected you to instruct us how to write it," Mr. MacVicar said.

"If your verdict is not guilty," the judge answered, "you…"

That is as far as he got.

"That is our verdict," said the foreman in a low voice.

The clerk indicated where the foreman was to write on the front of the warrant that had been served by Deputy Curtis to Sash in September.

"We the jury find the accused not guilty." Mr. MacVicar read the verdict aloud. An immediate outburst of applause got a reprimand from the judge. He sent officers into the courtroom to see that there was no disorder. With deliberate restraint, Judge Spratley sat at his bench until all had settled in the courtroom.

"The defendant will please rise."

Sash stood to hear the judge announce, "Dr. Kane, the jury has found you not guilty. You are free to go. Court is adjourned."

The judge sat back in his swivel chair. He was no longer hiding his feelings. He smiled as he watched the chaos before him. At his signal, photographers started shooting. Some climbed on chairs, the clerk's desk, the bench. Telegraph boys fell over each other. Sash was all but smothered by men and women crowding up to congratulate him on the outcome of the case.

Flanked by his father, his brother and his attorneys, Sash Kane made his way out of the Elizabeth City Courthouse—a free man. Reporters crowded around to get his comments.

"It was a terrible ordeal," Sash told them. "And I was mighty uncomfortable at times, although I am innocent and believed the jury would so find."

Sash said his immediate plans were to return to his post at the University of Tennessee. "Contrary to reports," he said, "I have not been asked to resign. There have not been difficulties between the authorities at the university and me. I retained a leave of absence until after the trial."

"How do you feel?"

"I feel vindicated. Completely vindicated. I could ask no more. I appealed for justice to the people of Virginia, which gave me my education and the wife I loved. I was given a fair, impartial trial and an intelligent, attentive jury sat in judgment on my case. Their verdict is such that the world will know."

"Will you come back to Virginia?"

"I expect to come here often to have a few moments alone at the side of my wife's grave."

"Will you see the Grahams?"

"Mrs. Graham was like a mother to me. I don't understand what she said in the courtroom, but I still love my wife's mother."

In answer to their questions, Sash said, "I bear no malice toward anybody."

The reporters caught up with some of the jurymen to question them about their deliberations. "The verdict of 'not guilty' tells our story," one of the twelve answered. "We've agreed to say no more."

One report on the street said the jury stood eight for acquittal and four for conviction on the first ballot. Another said it stood eleven to one for acquittal. No one on the jury would confirm the numbers.

Dorothy met the professor for lunch. He said he "didn't look forward to going back to Knoxville to break up our home there and arrange to move into other quarters." He spoke of possibly making a business trip to Philadelphia, but said he had no plans to visit Kane, Pennsylvania, in the immediate future. He was eager to get back to his teaching.

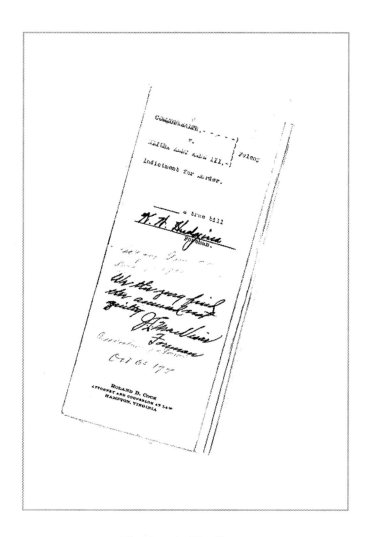

The Jury's Verdict

"I like teaching in a southern university. I admire the spirit of the students, especially their friendly relations with the faculty."

Sash told Dorothy, "I do not like to be termed a scholar. That smacks of pedantry, doesn't it?" he asked.

The conversation turned to his studies. "The Middle Ages fascinate me," he said. "I have lived in their literature for so long that it has become a part of me. Isn't it too bad there are so few people who appreciate that sort of thing?"

Then he answered his question, "No. I don't think so. It is good the world doesn't think too much about the past. It is so hopeless to think backward. The future brings progress."

Dorothy described Sash as

...a man withdrawn from humdrum existence. His mind dwells apart from the minds of ordinary men. He is a man of enormous enthusiasms and quick melancholies, of great emotion and abrupt coldness, of intricate ponderous thought and boyish naiveté.

Dorothy suggested the professor's enigmatic personality had made the charge against him possible.

He will always be a solitary figure, faintly mysterious."

The Old Acquaintances

"*M*olly! Molly Fredrick!" Molly heard her name shouted. When she turned, the man she saw calling after her didn't look like anyone she knew. *This is another reporter trying to find more background information on Sash, she thought. Haven't they had enough?* She frowned.

"What a sour face to greet an old acquaintance with!" Henry Landon said as he stepped in front of her.

"Why, Professor Landon," Molly responded, "Is this really you?"

"I think so," he quipped. "You may miss the bushy upper lip."

"Well, I do. You look so different. Ah…"

"One day I was talking, and I twisted the ugly thing right off my face," he joked of his old habit of fiddling with the ends of it.

"Well, let me see," said Molly as she studied his face. "I always knew there was a handsome man behind that masquerade."

"That remark gets you a free lunch," Henry responded. "Shall we go to the famous Hotel Chamberlin? I should like very much to get away from the crowds."

"Well," Molly said, "I haven't had a better offer… and I doubt seriously I will," she laughed. "Yes, that's sounds delightful."

"How long have you been here?" Henry asked.

"Since Monday. I was asked to come to testify, should they need me," Molly explained.

"You mean, the defense?" he asked.

"Sash's lawyers said they might need me to testify if the subject of Dreiser's book was brought up by the State."

"What could you have said?" Henry asked.

"They wanted me to tell them that Sash and I had discussed the movie versus the book. I would have certainly mentioned your name," Molly added.

"Oh? Why would you have said anything about me?"

"Because, my friend, I didn't want to be viewed like another "Betty" having an illicit affair with the professor of romance languages." Molly answered.

"I can see the headline now," Henry held one hand up to indicate the large print, "MOLLY FREDRICK, THE OTHER OTHER WOMAN."

"It's not funny, Henry. I was scared to death I might have to testify," Molly said. "The publicity could have cost me my job."

"Kane plans to go back to Knoxville. If they welcome him back, I'm sure you would have had no trouble."

"Sash says he's going back to the university, but that doesn't mean the university is going to take him back," Molly said.

"He was acquitted," Henry answered. "Don't you think that will take care of it?"

"It only means he didn't kill his wife, or if he did, they couldn't prove it. But the scandal about 'Betty' isn't going to be forgotten. He admitted having an affair with the woman. That doesn't look good for the university. I think he'll be asked to leave."

"Well, what do you think, Molly?" Henry asked, "Can a man be pressured to do something that is not in his nature to do?"

"Are we speaking of Sash now?"

"Perhaps. I don't know. I haven't been able to see that he was under any pressure to get rid of his wife. But you two got me interested in Dreiser's book."

"You read *An American Tragedy*?" Molly asked.

"I waded through it, you might say," Henry answered. "I thought I'd never get to the end, but this thing with Sash…"

"You mean it bothered you his wife ends up drowning right after we saw the movie with him?"

"Well, didn't it make you think… maybe?" Henry asked. "Was Sash Kane a Lothario and a bully, as his wife's people said, or was he the loving, attentive husband his friends said he was?"

"Sash has a way… ," Molly thought out loud, "that is, he doesn't mean for anyone to take him seriously. He flirts with all the women. He says things to shock people. He draws naughty pictures. What kind of nature does Sash have?"

"I found him likeable," Henry said.

"Yes, affable, but sometimes offensive."

"Well, he's certainly a gentleman," Henry asserted.

"Uh-huh. Sash is quite refined, though caddish," Molly said. "He's respectful, but abrupt. Polite, but vulgar. Anything we can say about Sash, we can also say the opposite."

"Then can we say he could have killed his wife, if we say he couldn't have?" Henry asked.

"Oh, gracious, no." Molly was quick to respond. "Sash enjoys toying with words. His mixed persona is his way of poking fun at folks who are too somber. Sash is an intellectual who refuses to be viewed as many of his contemporaries—a bunch of sedate stuffed shirts."

"How can we know what such a man is capable of?" Henry asked.

"Once I knew they might call me to testify, I stopped reading the newspapers," Molly said. "Was there something said in the trial that makes you wonder if Sash was guilty?"

"I wasn't there every day. I didn't hear what the Grahams said at first," Henry said. "But when they were brought back to testify a second time, they all seemed so determined to get Sash. Why were they so convinced he did it?"

"The jury wasn't convinced. The defense didn't even think it was necessary for me to testify. There was applause when the jury said 'not guilty.' The prosecution didn't have a shred of evidence."

"They didn't have to have proof," Henry said. "They were trying him on circumstantial evidence. They claimed that those letters the court wouldn't allow to be presented would have shown he was persuaded by his interest in 'Betty' to get rid of Jenny."

"When Sash took the stand," Molly said, "it must have been terrible for him."

"At first he looked uncomfortable, but once he told his story to his attorney, he was ready to answer anything the old prosecuting attorney from the big city threw at him. 'I loved the woman I couldn't save,' he said most convincingly. But then he did lose his temper once on the stand."

"Just imagine, being accused of killing the woman you loved," Molly said "and having to sit there while people say awful things. Who wouldn't lose his temper?"

"You could tell Sash's brother-in-law and his wife hated him," Henry said. "I didn't understand the whole thing about Sash and her brother. There was a disagreement over a motorcycle, and each told a different story of what had happened. Could that be why the man accused Sash of murder?

"Mr. Graham said that his daughter was devoted to him, but Sash claimed Jenny's father treated her badly," Henry said. "It's sad to think of all that sort of personal stuff being talked about for all to hear. And then Sash couldn't believe Mrs. Graham would say the things she said, for he always got along well with her. She had gone out to eat with Sash and Jenny lots of times, as well as the night before Jenny drowned. Sash said she was like a mother to him."

"One of my students came in to see me after the story appeared in the Knoxville newspaper," Molly said. "He was very upset they had charged Professor Kane with such a terrible crime."

"I think the news came as a shock to anyone who knew the man. It's hard to imagine someone you've been friendly with could kill another person."

"It was more than that," Molly answered. "Phil told me Sash had once told him that one day Phil would meet the right girl, and life would be wonderful. Sash told Phil he was married to the best girl in the world. Sash's students really liked him, and, I dare say, none of them thought he killed his wife."

"With a rather prestigious line of witnesses testifying the Kanes had an ideal marriage, the defense made the jurors wonder about the Grahams' accusations. People who had lived with him, above him, below him, and next door—educated people who could impress the court—all took their turns in the witness chair to say what a romantic, devoted couple Sash and Jenny were. Did you know her?" Henry asked.

"Jenny left the campus shortly after I came to know her. They invited a few of us over one evening in the early part of the semester. He played the violin, and she played the piano. They were most gracious hosts. She was very attractive and had a lovely voice," Molly answered.

"Yes, I heard her sing," Henry said, "But how were they as a couple? In court some people described them as lovebirds, but members of her family kept saying he treated her beastly."

"When I saw them together, I thought they had found the secret to staying in love," Molly remembered. "It's impossible for me to imagine Sash as a brute. I've heard Sash credited for vulgarity, but never for cruelty." Molly thought a minute. "I also heard he had a temper."

"He admitted that in court," Henry said. "He said he might have let go a 'healthy damn' every now and then."

"I am sure Sash can swear in every language known to man," Molly said. "If someone upset Sash, he could tear them apart with verbiage only he could understand. He's brilliant with languages and doesn't mind getting the better of the other fellow with words."

"Though Jenny's family accused him of swearing at her all night long," Henry said, "when Sash's attorney asked them why they didn't stop Sash, her father said he wouldn't do that. He said Sash was big enough to take both him and Jenny under his arm and toss them in the street. Mr. Graham said he never said anything to Jenny about her marriage, but...it seems to me, he also said he tried to get her to leave Sash. And can you believe Mr. Graham claiming he never heard his daughter complain of a heart attack?"

"Do you think the Grahams made up some of the stuff?"

"Could have. I don't know. It seems strange to me that her family were the only ones unaware of her heart troubles. Several people said they had seen her have an attack. She'd been to doctors all over and, if they didn't think she had heart problems, they at least said she thought so. Jenny's family members were the only ones who said Sash was cruel to Jenny. I think the Grahams' testimonies were so vengeful that they appeared to be out to get Sash at any cost. When you read the newspapers, you'll find some reporters thought so, too."

"What did you think of Sash's family?" Molly said.

"They were a force to tangle with. Dr. Kane and his other son, Thomas, were allowed to sit at the table with Sash. When the doctor was called to testify, he made certain he got to say what he'd come to say. It was something when Dr. Kane showed the jury the New Testament Sash had given him, insisting that Sash wasn't a 'godless man.'

"And then when Dr. Kane left the stand and turned to Judge Spratley and asked him to excuse him for taking so much time in testifying, saying 'I'm very interested in that little boy.' I thought the prosecutor was going to explode!

"Dr. Kane was rested and raring to go at it with the prosecutor that next day. If there was a favorite personality in the court," Henry told Molly, "it was Dr. Kane. He snapped back at the Commonwealth Attorney and got people laughing."

"Sash gets some of his spirit from his dad, I suppose," Molly said.

"You know about the old man?" Henry asked.

"You mean that he operated on himself? Of course. I think the first time I met Sash he said his name was "Elisha Kent, son of Evan O'Neill—who-took-out-his-own-appendix—Kane. But I'd forgotten about it until the drowning. I wonder if his father hadn't been so famous, if things would have played out differently."

"Of that you can be sure. But we'll never know how so," Henry answered. "That big building over there is the Chamberlin. Shall we go check out the bill of fare?" Henry was guiding Molly along.

"Did Sash ever tell you about his great-uncle Elisha?" he asked.

"When Sash was first arrested, I read about the famous explorer in the papers," Molly answered.

"Did you ever hear of the Fox sisters?" Henry whispered. They gave spiritual manifestations, or so they claimed. Well…"

The Languished Soul

*A*ccording to the court, the ordeal was over. Sash had been found not guilty. The trial had been like the circus come to town to entertain the public. While he rested in his hotel room, vandals invaded St. John's Cemetery and carried away the flowers that had been placed on Jenny's grave. The thieves had no respect for the dead and no understanding of Sash's quote from Dante: "There is no greater grief than to recall a happy time gone by in days of misery."

On Tuesday of the week after his acquittal, newspapers reported Sash's departure for Knoxville:

> After squaring accounts with the court of Hampton, receiving the congratulations of well-wishers on his acquittal and bidding farewell to his counsel, Dr. Elisha Kent Kane, III, left the Lower Virginia Peninsula as he turned westward toward Knoxville.

The article went on to say he was "to learn whether or not he is again to occupy his old chair as professor of romance languages."

The head of the university, President H. A. Morgan, referred all inquiries as to what the future held in store for Dr. Kane to Dean James Hoskins. Dean Hoskins refused to make any comment pending Dr. Kane's arrival in Knoxville.

Two days later Dean Hoskins met the press: "Dr. Kane came to my office last fall after he was arrested and released from prison and voluntarily tendered his resignation. We agreed that no announcement would be made until after the case was tried in order not to prejudice his case. He was to present his formal resignation after the trial, and he came to my office yesterday afternoon for that purpose. Professor Kane has relieved the university of a very delicate situation by tendering his formal resignation, which was accepted."

Sash was interviewed after the dean's announcement. "Gentlemen, the things that are news to you boys are stark tragedy to me," he managed a little smile for the eager newsmen. He said he didn't have any plans. "I am going to try, bit by bit, to rebuild my shattered life—just where, I don't know. I will have to gather the broken pieces and try to weave them back again. It means an entire reorganization of my life."

"Professor, what about Tennessee, do you feel they…"

"I have the deepest gratitude toward the administration and faculty of the university for their support," Sash said.

Back in Virginia, The *Newport News Daily Press* ran an editorial when the decision from Knoxville became known:

We can't be too careful about placing in jeopardy the life of a human being, for even if he be found innocent we can never return to him that which has been taken from him, nor compensate him for the anguish of the terrible ordeal to which he is subjected—wherever he goes there will be talk.

An editorial in The Newport News Star said:

Some men and women will always believe him guilty; others will have doubt, and none can forget the fact that he has been accused of being a wife murderer. Dr. Kane is a comparatively young man, yet he cannot possibly live long enough to overcome entirely the terrible blow that has been dealt his reputation.

Just as it was in Knoxville, the truth expressed by these editors could be found on the Virginia Peninsula and even in Sash's hometown of Kane. Sash believed the acquittal had proven his innocence, but many thought he and his lawyers had simply outsmarted the system. For some the headlines had suggested a plot by Sash and the "other woman" to kill Jenny Kane—the jury had clearly made the wrong decision. Judge Spratley hadn't wanted the Pennsylvanian convicted in his court, the Kane family money had paid for his acquittal. Even a man who argued Sash hadn't killed Jenny said that he was certain the man was glad to be rid of her.

It was reported the lettered professor had not received any offers from colleges or universities in the States, but that he was offered a position on the faculty of a European university. Another report quoted his saying that he would continue the study of romance languages at the University of Madrid in Spain. Confirmation of these reports could not be obtained.

He returned to Kane: Resting At Home.

Sash determined to spend the holiday season with his father and then decide what he could do with his "shattered life." Dr. Evan Kane was feeling ill since his trip to Virginia. He wanted Sash to stay in Kane and asked him to serve as the hospital administrator.

On the seventh of January, the old doctor operated on himself for an inguinal hernia. It was a rather dangerous operation. He used local anesthetic as he had used previously. The doctor was still making his case against putting a patient to sleep during an operation. Dr. Kane had to rely upon his sense of touch in reaching the affected parts.

It was reported he laughed and chatted throughout the operation. At one point, he coughed. He then remarked, "Now that was bad, very bad."

As he was wheeled from surgery, the tenacious Dr. Kane smiled and announced, though in a scant voice, "The operation was a success. Both patient and attending physician are doing good."

That was not to continue to be the case. In the early spring, the doctor, who had made great strides in the treatment of cancer patients, became stricken with pneumonia.

Gladys Schuler, a graduate of the nursing school at the Kane hospital, had worked with Dr. Kane as his nurse and was there at his side. She had been with him when he operated on himself. Dr. Kane had a great fondness for Gladys. Evan Kane knew his time had come. His "doctor" couldn't lie to him. He regretted he didn't have more time with Sash. "Take care of Sash for me," he told Gladys, knowing she already had special feelings for his little boy.

He and Sash laughed over the time when Sash had ridden his pony to the top floor of the manor house and how angry his father had been with him. Dr. Kane reminded Sash of the time he'd come to the dinner table with his arm all swollen. When Evan examined it, he found Sash had given himself a tattoo with India ink, and it had become infected. The childish misdemeanors of a boy were now the source of laughter for the father and son. But, more than that, Evan and Sash expressed their admiration for each other. With their characteristically cunning personalities, it had been difficult for either to allow the other to have the last word. Now they regretted they had not recognized how much they were alike all along.

On the first of April, just three months after Sash's acquittal, Evan Kane died.

Sash married Gladys Schuler in 1934. Like Jenny, Gladys was enamored with Sash, and he with her. They turned the old family Manor House, built in 1896 by plans Sash's grandfather drew up before his death, into a wayside inn. The family had called the house "Anoatok," an Eskimo name meaning "a wind-loved spot."

It was truly a cold and windy place in the winter, but the Manor House Inn was a delightful destination for summer vacationers. An amazing collection of war relics and memorabilia were on display throughout the manor. Treasures from the arctic, the explorer's presentation sword, guns and helmets collected by Kane men participating in various conflicts over the centuries, and wonderful art pieces, many of which were done by family members, amazed and enchanted the guests.

On the roof was a huge black crow weathervane that Sashy made for the Inn.

In the two dining rooms, Gladys used the family's Limoges china to serve her guests. One room was called the "Bucktail Room" after Thomas Kane's Union regiment. A huge painting of "A Ship and Icebergs" by James Hamilton hung in the main hall over a tremendous fireplace. Two Civil War percussion pistols served as the knob on the stairway post.

Sash put a name on each guestroom and painted an eight-to-ten inch character on the door to represent the name. On the "Summer Room" he had a lady wearing overalls, a garden hat and gloves holding a rake and a watering can. On the "Antique Room" he put a man slumbering with his feet sticking out past the foot of the four-poster bed. The "Sunset Room" had a girl in a bathing suit, brightly colored sombrero-sized hat, with high heels on her feet. There were eleven guestrooms on the first and second floors, beautifully furnished, offering lovely accommodations for people who came to explore the Alleghenies, or go hunting.

The wisdom of the Kane family was emblazoned on mantles and over doors. "Life is like iron. Use it. It wears away. Use it not. It rusts away," was engraved in gold on the white mantle in the living room. On the front steps the words, "Nothing ventured—Nothing gained" greeted the guests.

For the remainder of his life, Hobo, the German Shepherd, had a doghouse in the yard of the Manor House Inn. The plaque over his door said, "USELESS AND WORTHLESS BUT ABSOLUTELY PRICELESS." He wasn't a Hollywood star, but he got good billing, and the guests at the inn thought he should have been in movies. He was a handsome dog.

Sash found amusement in digging out the cellar pub, knowing his Grandmother Bessie, who had had the manor built, would shudder at the thought. Bessie had been a staunch disciplinarian on the subject of drinking alcohol. Sash felt no shame. He painted over her WCTU pin in her portrait and opened a very popular rathskeller. He covered its walls with ribald watercolors that would make the women blush. He made five tree-slab tables and decorated them with risqué World War I caricatures.

There was a party every night with Clayton Johnson, the bartender, doing double duty at the piano. There would be singing and dancing until some early-to-bed guest would complain of the noise. The flamboyant host circulated all about the manor making certain everyone felt welcomed and had every comfort he could offer them. Once someone had enjoyed the hospitality of Gladys and Sash Kane at the inn, they were sure to return.

The couple made the third floor of the manor house their home. There was nothing ostentatious about their quarters. They surrounded themselves with everything they loved—books, pictures, maps and a telescope to study the brilliant stars in the dark skies above this remote part of Pennsylvania. Sash built a peculiar fireplace on the third floor—mostly of brick but distressed with odd stones protruding like barnacles on ocean rocks. The words on his fireplace said: "He Is Not Fit to Live Who Is Afraid to Die."

Sash and Gladys had two children, a boy and a girl, who would grow up unaware of the trial in Virginia and how it had forced a brilliant professor to become an innkeeper. Sash only told them, "I want you to know, I have never done anything dishonorable."

The US Army called Sash back into active duty in World War II. He served in the 856th Battalion. He retired a colonel. He returned home with malaria and, shortly afterwards, suffered a crippling stroke. He would spend the next thirteen years bedridden while his family continued, with as many as twelve employees, to operate the inn in the summer months. In the winter they would take Sash to Florida where they rented a palm tree log cabin.

Sash died in 1959. He is buried in Clearwater, Florida.

Elisha Kent Kane, III, with his second wife and children.

—*Courtesy of the Kane Family*

Epilogue

You may conclude, though my subjects took the road to Justice, they ended up somewhere else. The jury found Elisha innocent, but the stigma of having been accused a wife-murderer remained with him. The woman, so afraid of death that she possibly hastened her own, was publicly portrayed as a pathetic hypochondriac when she quite possibly had a legitimate ailment. And, for all who grieved her passing, the time of mourning was vandalized by the unsavory publicity, just as surely as her grave was by those who stole the flowers.

Author's Notes

The Back River Light was decommissioned in 1936. Twenty years later, Hurricane Flossy destroyed what was left of the little brick lighthouse. Only a pile of stones, out from the shore, mark the place where Jenny drowned. Grandview, its beach and marshes, is a wildlife preserve, making it as isolated as it was when Jenny and Sash went there to have their picnics. A screaming voice cannot be distinguished as male, or female, or maybe even seagulls squawking. A boater is unaware of a beachcomber; the beachcomber unaware of him. River rocks and seashells collect upon the beach in mounds as the waves have deposited them. A rusty crab pot, a sea-green rope, the stumps of trees long felled by the water's washing dot the shore. Just outside the limits of the preserve, modern housing units line up to newly made streets, and an historic marker in a turnaround tells that "One mile north, the Back River Lighthouse stood for 127 years."

The house where the Grahams lived is still standing. It is used as an office. Hilton, a part of Newport News, still has its charming "village" houses. After the trial, Jenny's parents moved into her brother's home in Phoebus. Mr. Graham went to work for L.M. Newcomb where Hop worked. Hop eventually became the vice president and treasurer of the company. The big news story of 1947 on the Peninsula was the fire that destroyed the Newcomb plant. The fire of undetermined origin sprang up quickly in the early hours of July 30. A small article in the newspaper less than a week later told of the suicide death of Walter Hopkins (Hop) Graham:

> It is thought that the fire... in the Newcomb plant last week preyed on his mind and led to the act which cost his life.

Dr. Paul Parker, the coroner, "pronounced the case as one of unmistakable suicide."

The red brick courthouse where Elisha Kane was tried was painted white by the WPA in 1940, but is still in use. There is no

Elizabeth City County though; the city lines of Hampton and Newport News meet. The jail where Elisha was held was demolished in 1972. Time has not worn away the inscription on Jenny's tombstone in the historic Old St. John's Church Cemetery.

Judge Spratley was named to the Virginia State Supreme Court in 1936 where he served until he retired to work his rose garden. When asked if he enjoyed trial court work more than his service at the appellate level, he admitted trial court was sometimes more interesting. "You don't get the interest and humor and the play of emotions in a writ that you do when you actually try a case."

Percy Carmel and Frank Kearney remained the best of friends. Percy stayed with his law practice, taking more interest in helping younger lawyers get a start than in promoting himself. He never married, but was a favorite member of the family and the community. He always had a cat. It was always black, and he named them all "Midnight."

Frank married. He was later named Judge of the 11th Judicial Circuit Court in Elizabeth City County. Participation in the biggest murder trial of the century helped establish the reputations of both attorneys as he had predicted it would.

There were possibly more Hiram Smiths in Richmond, Virginia, than there were Elisha Kanes in Kane, Pennsylvania. The "Harry" Smith who worked on the prosecution in the Kane murder trial was the son of a wealthy inventor and manufacturer by the same name. The attorney's oldest son was also given the name. It was noted Harry left Hampton immediately after giving his closing remarks at the Kane murder trial. He didn't stay for the verdict.

Molly Fredrick and Henry Landon are fictitious characters. All other names in this book were taken from court records, newspaper articles and interviews. The arguments given by the Commonwealth and defense attorneys are as they presented them. The bizarre remarks of the defendant and witnesses were copied from the record. The testimony of the coroner is just as he stumbled through it.

The Book of Good Love of the Archpriest of Hita, Gongerism and the Golden Age, American Tragedy, Isadora Duncan's autobiography and *the Autobiography Written with Complete Dishonesty* are all published works, though "rare." The correspondence between Sash and Jenny was kept in the Virginia State Records, and the infamous B.H.D. letter was published for all to read.

The Kane family sold the Manor House in 1983. To this date it remains an inn. The ambiance of the place may at first seem very different. Still the history of a great family, a family of doctors, lawyers and heroes, belongs to the house.

Dorothy Ducas became good friends with Eleanor Roosevelt. During World War II she was named Chief of the Magazine Division of the War Information Bureau. She was recognized by the W.I.C. (Women in Communications) in 1943 for her outstanding work.

When Dorothy Ducas interviewed Elisha Kane on the day of his acquittal, he said, "The freedom of opportunity—mental freedom, not moral license—is the most valuable thing on earth." Though freed from the charge of murder against him, he would never be free of suspicion. He would never again experience what had been for him the most valuable thing on earth.